Coventry Patmore

Religio poetæ etc

Coventry Patmore

Religio poetæ etc

ISBN/EAN: 9783741157820

Manufactured in Europe, USA, Canada, Australia, Japa

Cover: Foto ©Andreas Hilbeck / pixelio.de

Manufactured and distributed by brebook publishing software (www.brebook.com)

Coventry Patmore

Religio poetæ etc

RELIGIO POETÆ

ETC.

BY

COVENTRY PATMORE

NEW EDITION

LONDON
GEORGE BELL AND SONS, YORK STREET
COVENT GARDEN
1898

PREFACE

"SOME of these Essays have already appeared in the *Fortnightly Review* or elsewhere."

In the original issue the author had noted that "thoughts had sometimes been repeated, almost in the same words." In the rearrangement here adopted no attempt has been made to obviate this repetition, which may be even more conspicuous than in the original order; but, "as these thoughts are mostly unfamiliar and significant, readers will be none the worse for encountering them twice or even thrice."

Shortly before his death, Mr. Patmore had suggested a rearrangement for a new issue, which has been adopted and completed for this edition. A few corrections and omissions have also been made, the greater number of which were either marked or sanctioned by the author himself. The alterations not actually his own are few and of small importance.

Some obvious mistakes in matters of fact, and some errors of punctuation, have been corrected; here and there a word has been transposed where the original order was imperfect; and one or two passages which seemed to have been written for an immediate purpose rather than for more permanent effect have been omitted.

CONTENTS

ESSAY	PAGE
I. Religio Poetæ	1
II. The Precursor	10
III. The Language of Religion	18
IV. Attention	31
V. Christianity an Experimental Science	38
VI. "A People of a Stammering Tongue"	46
VII. The Bow set in the Cloud	51
VIII. Christianity and "Progress"	57
IX. Simplicity	64
X. Ancient and Modern Ideas of Purity	68
XI. Conscience	73
XII. Real Apprehension	77
XIII. Seers, Thinkers, and Talkers	85
XIV. Possibilities and Performances	96
XV. Imagination	102

ESSAY	PAGE
XVI. THE LIMITATIONS OF GENIUS	108
XVII. A "PESSIMIST" OUTLOOK	113
XVIII. THOUGHTS ON KNOWLEDGE, OPINION, AND INEQUALITY	121
XIX. LOVE AND POETRY	139
XX. THE WEAKER VESSEL	147
XXI. DIEU ET MA DAME	159

I

RELIGIO POETÆ

No one, probably, has ever found his life permanently affected by any truth whereof he has been unable to obtain a *real apprehension*, which, as I have elsewhere shown, is quite a different thing from real *comprehension*. Intellectual assent to truths of faith, founded on what the reason regards as sufficient authority for, at least, experimental assent, must, of course, precede real apprehension of them, as also must action, in a sort experimental, on faith of truths so assented to; but such faith and action have little effective life, and are likely soon to cease, or to become mere formalities, unless they produce some degree of vital *knowledge* or *perception*. I do not see what is to become of popular Religion, parodied and discredited as Christianity is by the "Religions" of Atheists, Moralists, Formalists, Philanthropists, Scientists, and Sentimentalists, unless there can be infused into it some increased longing and capacity for real apprehension.

Coleridge, at one time, proposed to write a "Religio Poetæ," with the view, I suppose, of correcting the imperceptive character of modern faith. The Poet is, *par excellence*, the *perceiver*, nothing having any interest for him, unless he can, as it were, see and touch it with the spiritual senses, with which he is pre-eminently endowed. The Saints, indeed, seem, for the most part, to have had these senses greatly developed by their holiness and their habitual suppression of the corporeal senses. But, as a rule, they do not speak, perhaps from the fear of being too implicitly believed; or, if they do, they are careful

"To make Truth look as near a lie
As can comport with her divinity,"

in order to adapt it to the public capacity. But the Poet has this advantage, that none, save the few whose ears are opened to the teaching which would be ridiculed or profaned to their own destruction by the many, will think that he is in earnest, or that his flights into regions of perception, in which they can perceive nothing, are other than flights of fancy. He occupies a quite peculiar position—somewhere between that of a

Saint and that of Balaam's Ass. His intellect seems capable of a sort of independent sanctification, while his moral constitution usually enables him to prophesy without a Prophet's responsibilities. The Saint dreads lest he should receive praise of men for the holiness through which he has acquired his knowledge; the Poet understands very well that no one will or ought to think the better of his righteousness for his being a seer.

The Poet, again, is not more singular for the delicacy of his spiritual insight, which enables him to see celestial beauty and substantial reality where all is blank to most others, than for the surprising range and alertness of vision, whereby he detects, in external nature, those likenesses and echoes by which spiritual realities can alone be rendered credible and more or less apparent, or subject to "real apprehension," in persons of inferior perceptive powers. Such likenesses, when chosen by the imagination, not the fancy, of the true Poet, are *real* words—the only real words; for "that which is unseen is known by that which is seen," and natural similitudes often contain and are truly the visible *ultimates* of the unseen. "God," says Goethe, "is manifested in ultimates,"—a doctrine destined to produce some amazing developments of Christianity, which is yet in its infancy, though it seems, as it has always seemed to contemporaries, to be in its decay. The Poet, again, has, like Newton, a special *calculus*—a doctrine of infinite series, whereby he attains to unveil the infinite and express it in credible terms of the finite, showing it, if not as actually apprehensible, yet as possibly, and even certainly so, to orders of intellect which are probably only a continuation and development of our own. Of this *calculus* Dante has abundantly made use, and those passages in his Poems which we read with the most passionate delight and real apprehension are precisely those in which the argument rises from natural experience to the dizziest heights of spiritual probability. For neither in this, nor in any other Poet of like rank, is there any solution of continuity between the lowest and the highest, any more than there is in the progress of the seed from its first germination through its various transformations in seed-leaf, stem, flower, and fruit. It is still nature, but more mature nature—nature developed by successive and intelligible degrees of growth and glory, the first of these degrees being, even in this life, quite familiar to those who *know* the truth of Wordsworth's saying—

"By grace divine,
Not otherwise, O Nature, are we thine."

Again, the Poet always treats spiritual realities

as the concrete and very credible things they truly are. He has no slipshod notions about the immeasurable and "infinite." He knows, as Plato knew, that God Himself is most falsely described as infinite. God is the synthesis, as Proclus declares in his treatise on the Fables of Homer, of "Infinite" and "Boundary," and is excellently intelligible, though for ever unutterable, by those who love Him.

Another vast advantage in the Poet's mode of teaching is that it is, even in its indignant denials of negation, necessarily and always, as far as he is a Poet, affirmative and positive. "Let your communication be, Yea, Yea, and Nay, Nay, for whatsoever is more than this cometh of evil." He gives the world to eat only of the Tree of Life, reality; and will not so much as touch the Tree of Knowledge, as the writer of Genesis ironically calls the Tree of Learning that leads to denial of knowledge. He is the very reverse of a "scientist." He is all vision and no thought, whereas the other is all thought and no vision. But "Where there is no vision the People perish"; and of thought without vision it may be truly said, "Dust shalt thou eat all the days of thy life," and "dust thou art and to dust shalt thou return." The Poet could not do other than he does. All realities will sing, but nothing else will. Judge then how much reality there is, in the modern teaching of religion, by the songs of its prophets! Where in these songs is the flavour of reality, "the sweetness of the lips that increaseth learning "?

There is a kind of perception in a state of solution which must not be overlooked or depreciated. It is the substance of most of the finest lyric poetry, and of the religion of nearly all religious people, especially in these days. But this fire-mist is a very inferior form of perceptive knowledge. There is none of it in Dante. It is the "Infinite" without the "Bound," and is not sufficiently concrete to be very serviceable or communicable, being mainly unintelligent heat, though that heat may be holy. For effective teaching there must be the disc of really apprehended dogma; rays diversely reflected and refracted from clouded sources will not do. The soul *dares* not believe its own marvellous guesses and instincts, unless it can fall back upon definite dogma for confirmation and justification, nor can the corollaries of dogma, which are often of far more personal weight than dogma itself, be inferred without a definite premise.

I suppose I need not say that by Poets I do not, in this argument, mean only or chiefly those who have written in verse. During most of the centuries which have elapsed since the beginning of Christianity the highest imaginative as well as intellectual powers of mankind have been wholly absorbed by theology and theological psychology; and I may say, without fear of contradiction from those who are at all well read in the works of St. Augustine, St. Bernard, St. Thomas Aquinas, St. Francis of Sales, St. John of the Cross, and a score of others like them, that the amount of substantial poetry, of imaginative insight into the noblest and loveliest reality to be found in their writings, is ten times greater than is to be found in all the poets of the past two thousand years put together. The vastness of the mass hinders our appreciation of its substance and altitude. Aquinas is to Dante as the Tableland of Thibet is to the Peak of Teneriffe; and the first is not less essentially a poet, in the sense of a Seer, because his language is even more austere and without ornament, than that of the latter. It is true that the outward form of poetry is an inestimable aid to the convincing and persuasive power of poetical realities; but there is a poetic region—the most poetical of all—which is incapable of taking the form of poetry. Its realities take away the breath which would, if it could, go forth in song; and there is such a boundless wilderness of equally inspiring subject to choose from that choice becomes impossible, and the tongue of love and joy is paralysed.

To conclude, I think that it must be manifest to fitly qualified observers, that religion, which to timid onlookers appears to be on a fair way to total extinction, is actually, both by tendency from within and compulsion from without—through heresies and denials of all that cannot be "realised"—in the initial stage of a new development, of which the note will be *real apprehension*, whereby Christianity will acquire such a power of appeal to the "pure among the Gentiles," *i.e.* our natural feelings and instincts, as will cause it to appear almost like a New Dispensation, though it will truly be no more than the fulfilment of the express promises of Christ and His Apostles to the world,—promises which in every age have been fulfilled to thousands and thousands of individuals who have so learned "the King's secret" as to have become the converts of intelligible joy. Or would it be too vast a hope that such a development may truly assume the proportions and character of a New Dispensation, the Dispensation of the Holy Spirit, the Spirit of Life and perceived Reality, continuing and fulfilling the Dispensation of Christ, as His did that of the Father—the "Persona," or aspect of the Holy Trinity in the worship of the Israelites? a Dispensation under which millions instead of thousands should awake to those facts of life of which Christ said, "I have many things to say to you, but you cannot bear them yet; but when the Holy Spirit shall come, He shall teach you the things I have told you." Under the first dispensation men were the servants of God; under the second, His sons: "Sons now we are of God, but what we shall be hath not yet appeared." What if, under a third, "the voice of the Bride and the Bridegroom shall be heard again in our streets"? Our Lord, by an intervention which He declared to be premature, converted water into the wine of the Marriage Feast. He did so for hundreds, before the time of His manifestation in the flesh; He has done so for thousands who "have lived to see His coming" since. What if His fuller coming to the whole Church should be a like revelation, even in this life, for every one who so "seeks first the kingdom of God and His righteousness," that "all these things shall be added to him"?

II

THE PRECURSOR

ST. AUGUSTINE, in answer to some one who objected that there were several interpretations of a passage in Scripture besides that which the Saint had offered, replied: "The more interpretations the better." The words of Scripture and of the ancient mythologies and profoundest Poets may, indeed, be credited with containing and intending all the truths which they can be made to carry, and I do not mean to controvert any other account of the significance of the peculiar, mysterious, and, in *the letter*, unaccountable place held by St. John the Baptist in relation to the gospel of Divine Love, when I point out that the relation of Natural Love to Divine Love is represented by him with a consistent aptness and an amount of detail which can scarcely have been accidental.

In the first place he is represented not as

simply a Prophet, but as the "*Precursor*" of Christ, as Natural Love is the Precursor of the Divine. "The natural first, and afterwards the spiritual." St. Bernard says: "The love of God has its first root in the most secret of the human affections." The love between God and the soul is constantly declared to be, in its highest perfection, the love that subsists between Bridegroom and Bride ("thy Maker is thy Husband," etc., etc.), and our only means of understanding and attaining to these supernatural relations are the meditation and contemplation of their types in nature. "The unseen is known by that which is seen." "No greater than He was born of woman," *i.e.* nature; but "the least in the Kingdom of Heaven," *i.e.* Divine Love, "is greater than he"; and, as the latter increases, he must decrease. His baptism was necessary even to Christ as the representative of Christians, for none can receive effectually Christ's baptism of fire and the Holy Spirit without the previous baptism of the purifying water of natural love,—water itself always signifying, in the parabolic vocabulary of all primitive religions, the life of the external senses, or nature. Food of locusts, *wild* honey, and clothing of camel's hair are also interpreted,—by those who are most learned in that mystical vocabulary which everybody acknowledges to have been largely in use by the writers of the Scriptures as well as by those of all the great mythologies, and without which a great part of Scripture is hopelessly unintelligible,—as significant of life in natural good, of which the highest is natural love. "Honey," writes one of the most deeply learned in this vocabulary, "signifies natural good." "Locusts," says the same writer, "signify nutriment in the extreme natural," and camel's hair and a leathern girdle "denote what is natural," skin and hair being those things which are most external. St. John the Baptist is spoken of by the Church as the "strong man" and the "standard-bearer," being the mightiest of human powers and their leader. He alone of all natural men is "sanctified from his mother's womb" and originally holy: "sole mortal thing of worth immortal." He "came to bear testimony to the light" of that Love which is the fulfilment of the prophecy of natural love. Herod, the world, was friendly to him, who nevertheless rebuked the Tetrarch for his violation of a law of natural love, and the Saint was sacrificed by him to an impure passion and the allurements of a dancing girl; which is the usual fate of pure natural love, "sanctified from the womb," when brought into conflict with the sensuality which apes and profanes it. "Let the Church," says the Service of the Saint's Day, "rejoice in the nativity of blessed John the Baptist, by whom she came to the knowledge of the Author of her regeneration." "Behold," says the same Service, "I have given thee to be the light of the *Gentiles*," *i.e.* the interpreter of the faculties and desires of the *natural* man. In virtue of his peculiar mission the Baptist compares and measures himself with Christ as no other ever did: "He must increase, I must decrease"; "He cometh, the latchet of whose shoes I am not worthy to unloose;" I am not the Christ, that *most* holy love, for whom ye, who have not yet seen Him, take me, but only the one pure mortal voice "crying in the desert" of the world, and prophesying of Him; "I ought to be baptized by Thee, and comest Thou to me?" "He was not the true light, but was to give testimony of the light." "After me there cometh a man who is preferred before me," etc.

Jesus, being baptized by John, the heavens were opened to him, and a voice from heaven said: "This is my beloved Son, in whom I am well pleased;" *i.e.* by the baptism of natural love, the heavens are *sensibly* opened to him who is already the Son of God, and Christ, as the representative of Christians, is declared then most pleasing to the Father when He has donned and assumed to Himself the *natural* life of love. Concerning the Baptist, our Lord afterwards says: "What went ye out to see? A prophet? Yea, I tell you, and *more than a prophet*. For this is he of whom it is written, Behold I send my *Angel* before thy face, who shall prepare thy way before thee," "and if you will receive it, he is Elias that is to come. *He that hath ears, let him hear.*" Our Lord says of John: "If I bear witness of myself, my witness is not true" (that is, the Divine Love cannot effectually witness directly of itself), "there is another" (natural love) "that beareth witness of me. He was a burning and a shining light, and you were willing for a time to rejoice in him." John is "the *friend* of the Bridegroom, who standeth and heareth Him, and rejoiceth with joy because of the Bridegroom's voice. This *my joy is therefore fulfilled.*" John, though naturally nearer to Jesus than any other man "born of woman" (nature) "knew him not" but by the coming of the Holy Spirit, *i.e.* divine inspiration. So natural love, though so pure an image of the divine, knows not the divine until this is supernaturally revealed to it.

What seems to be thus obscurely shown forth as a parable in the life of the Precursor is, however, plainly affirmed by other parts of Scripture and by the doctrine of the Church concerning the significance of natural love. It is distinctly declared to be a "great Sacrament," or fact having a symbolic value of the highest consequence, as representative of the final and essentially nuptial relationship of Christ and the Church, of which every member is a church in little, with Our Lord for her head, as man is the head of woman, and God the Head of Christ. It is remarkable that, in a time when general reverence for religion is greatly diminishing, a true but altogether unenlightened reverence for the holy mystery of natural love should be sensibly increasing among us; and we may, perhaps, hail this circumstance as the precursor of a new development of Christianity which shall exert a hitherto unknown power over men, as being based upon and explanatory of their universal instincts and longings, which the symbol is, by as universal consent, wholly incapable of satisfying. And, besides the interest of the feelings, the intellect of man, which is now bent upon examining everything, must find, in the otherwise inexplicable phenomena of natural love, a satisfaction in the prospect of finding its key in another mystery which is, at least, much less inscrutable and does not involve any of the anomalies and absurdities of that passion, when it is regarded as an end having no further end. Every one who has loved and reflected on love for an instant, knows very well that what is vulgarly regarded as the end of that passion, is, as the Church steadfastly maintains, no more than its accident. The flower is not for the seed, but the seed for the flower. And yet what is that flower, if it be not the rising bud of another flower, flashed for a moment of eternal moment before our eyes, and at once withdrawn, lest we should misunderstand the prophecy, and take it for our final good? If it be other than a symbol, that is, as Coleridge defines a symbol to be, a part taken to represent the whole, then love, which the heart of every lover knows to be the supreme sanity, must be condemned by the intellect as the supreme insanity; and its "extravagances," which, from the Church's point of view, are in the highest representative order, must be looked upon as those of a maniac who takes a green goose for a goddess and himself for a god. But all this becomes clear when the parties to love are regarded as priest and priestess to one another of the divine womanhood and the divine manhood which are inherent in original Deity. They are but ministers to each other of the "great sacrament" of that glory "which the Son had with the Father before the beginning of the world"; and the co-existence of the greatest defects, short of an absolute defect of manhood and womanhood, with a claim to the greatest reverence and devotion, has its exact analogue in the nature and claims of priesthood, as being the vehicle—and only the vehicle—of the Divine in sacramental administrations.

I should far exceed the space to which I have desired to limit myself were I to exhaust the sayings of the Scripture and the services of the Church which bear upon this interpretation of the Precursorship of John. Let me, however, point out that the great painters of the Renaissance, from Botticelli and earlier downwards—men who show, to those who have eyes to see, the most ardent interest in the hidden meanings of scriptural sayings and events,—seem to have discerned and intended to convey the substance of what I have now said, by their frequent associations of the *two* Johns, John the Baptist and John "the *Divine*," as companions and co-worshippers of the Child Jesus, their synthesis, "God made Man of the Woman," to whose maternal bosom he eternally clings.

III

THE LANGUAGE OF RELIGION

THE realities discerned by faith are susceptible of infinite corroboration, for "God is infinitely visible and infinitely credible," and, since the knowledge of God is the one end of life, the sum of human wisdom consists in the accumulation of such corroborations. Now any fresh and original testimony is thus corroborative. It is the nature of man to believe the more because another believes, and to derive additional knowledge from another's mode of knowing. But how shall such testimony be conveyed, without betraying knowledge which often cannot be attempted to be spoken without profanation by and peril to the ignorant, except in enigmas which are clear to those who know, but hopelessly dark to those who do not? Accordingly we find that the teaching of every great religion, the Jewish and Christian perhaps above all, when it once leaves the preparatory stage of natural religion and morals and formal dogma, becomes mainly enigmatical and mythical. It is quite right that popular teaching should be limited, as it is, to the preparatory stage and to the enforcement of it by Divine sanction, threats, and general promises; for the house of God must be built, the soul must know the direction in which to look for light, and must be formed gradually into sincere desire of and constant endeavour for perfection, before God can inhabit it, and baptize it with that fire without which the baptism of water lies dormant as a grain of wheat in an Egyptian tomb. It is at this point that *real religion, which is self-evident,* begins, and at this point occurs that great change in the mode of the soul's progress which is well known to Catholic psychologists. Up to this point the progression is from truth to good; afterwards from good to truth, its rule then becoming "prove all things; hold fast" (not "that which is true," but) "that which is good"; the substance becomes the guide to the form, whereas, before, the form was the guide to the substance; and at this point the Church begins to teach the soul, chiefly by enigmas, how she may best understand the instructions and reciprocate the complacencies of that Divine Lover of whom she is henceforward the intimate companion and the living abode.

THE LANGUAGE OF RELIGION

The *fact* of the existence of these enigmas lies patent to the dullest. The vision of Ezechiel (which no one was permitted to read before he was thirty years of age), Seir and Paran, in which God was, but the people knew it not; the myth given in the Breviary on the day of the "apparition of St. Michael"; the great serpent, Leviathan; the King of Egypt become King of Israel; the almost identical myth of Proteus, the sea-beast, also called "Cetes, King of Egypt"; the birth of Aphrodite; the mystery of Persephone, whose true name it was not lawful to utter, concerning which Æschylus says: "Happy is he who comprehends it, for over him Hades shall have no power"; and a thousand other such things are manifest "riddles," and were manifestly meant for such. Moreover, they are, for the most part, such *elaborate* riddles that the key which unlocks any one of them, the thought which fills up all the manifold vacuities of external sense, must be *the* key and *the* thought.

Of most such enigmas Proclus says, in his treatise on the Fables of Homer, that they are unfit for the reading of youth, to whom they are absurd, or scandalous, or worse; but that they are the proper food of age when purged by discipline from obscuring and uncontrolled passions, the co-existence of which with the knowledge of

Divine secrets would involve that conjunction of perceived good with its denial by actual evil, which is more irremediably fatal to the soul than any amount of unmixed impurity. The senseless and often repulsive external word of these enigmas is as the black "veil of Moab," which God hangs before the sanctuaries of His brightest glory; and as the foul expirations of the serpent of Cos, which repelled all but him who was pure and bold enough in faith to kiss the death-breathing lips, and so convert them into those of a goddess, exhaling celestial perfumes.

Her whole system of language and rites proves either that the Church, who can speak her mind plainly enough when there is occasion for plainness, wantonly and habitually indulges in the folly of delivering a large part of her message in a language that few can understand, or that there is a body of knowledge which ought not to be and cannot be effectually communicated to all; and that, in her reticence, she is but obeying the command: "Tell not the vision to any man till Christ be risen" in him.

It would, no doubt, be of great use to many if the meaning of a few of the principal of the symbolic words common to all great religions were made a part of religious instruction; though it is wonderful how, by a sort of instinct, some of these keys are discerned and read by the simplest and least instructed of those who, among their low surroundings and labours, lead pure and meditative lives. I have heard some of our "savages," haunters of "Little Bethels," "Sions," and "Carmels," use the obscurest imagery of Scripture with an evident grasp of significance which many a Bishop might have envied. Such acquaintance with the vocabulary of symbols would not unveil anything which ought to remain veiled, while the ordinary reader and unenlightened enthusiast would be saved by it from the absurdities and scruples and often pernicious extravagances into which he now falls through his literal adoption of words which to sensible persons are manifestly parabolic; and the student of deeper capacity would be provided with the clues without which he cannot read even the letter of the enigmas of life.

To readers of the early Christian writers, the interpretation of many of these words must be familiar. The names of the four chief points of the compass, water, fire, cloud, thunder, lightning, nation, generation, father, mother, son, daughter, rich, poor, tree, stone, fish, mountains, birds, rod, flower, leaf, etc., etc., have fixed significances without the knowledge of which thousands of passages of Scripture, even those not involving any enigmatic meaning, cannot be understood. What, without such knowledge, can be made of passages, among innumerable others, like this: "The coming of the Son of Man is as the lightning which shineth from the east unto the west; for where the body is there shall the eagles be gathered together"? Or how, without such means of interpretation, can some of the direct injunctions of Our Lord, even in what is vulgarly supposed to be the plain speaking of the Sermon on the Mount, be obeyed? Of some of these injunctions, St. Augustine, rejecting the literal sense, says, in one of his sermons: "You may do these things if you can, but I cannot." From what torments might the poor simpleton of a modern pietist be saved by remembering that Our Lord "spake not without a parable"!

This mode of expressing realities by *things* having some resemblance to them, carried to the highest and fully conventionalised in the Egyptian hieroglyphic writing, was, no doubt, the origin of the similar language of Scripture, the early Church, and the mythologists, and must have been readily intelligible by the learned and those *mystæ* to whom their learning was gradually imparted. A still earlier mode of what may be called real speech may be found in those first roots of language which William Barnes and other philologists have shown to constitute a system of *phonetic* imagery —of sounds having a subtle correspondence to things. And the language of the poetry—the only *real* speech—of all nations and times, has largely consisted of a mixture of phonetic and objective imagery.

There is, besides, the more spacious imagery of parable proper, of which the external word is a consistent story, fictive or actually historic. Of this kind it may be well to point out that the Church, in her services, authorises the belief that many of the simplest incidents, even in the New Testament, have parabolic meanings of far higher value than the historic, which meanings we are sometimes called upon, in the prayers that, in the Breviary, etc., follow the recitals, to beg that "we may be made worthy to understand." Indeed, nothing can account for the emphasis and repetition with which some, extremely trivial, incidents are related in the New Testament, without attributing to the writers either the extreme of silliness and irrelevance, or a wisdom of which few of us are worthy to lift the veil.

Let it be remarked that symbolic and more or less enigmatic language and rites have a high value, even when they are not intended to conceal truth from those to whom its expression would be premature. They compel, in the recipient of their teaching, a state of active co-operation, a voluntary excitement of the mind, greatly more favourable to the abiding effect of moral truths and impressions than is the state of merely passive attention. This mode of reception includes the act of reflection, without which no knowledge ever becomes our own. And here let it be said that, so far are the originators and doctors of the great religions of the world and its greatest poets from having adopted an unnatural method of teaching, that it is the very method of Nature, whose book, from beginning to end, is nothing but a series of symbols, enigmas, parables, and rites, only to be interpreted by the "discerning intellect of man" actively and laboriously employed.

The rites, customs, architecture, ornaments, and vestures of the Church are stores of more or less enigmatic teaching, and not one can be destroyed or altered without risk of some unknown loss. What have we not lost, what loss have we not to fear in the future, from the vandalism of "good taste." How "natural," for example, it would be that King Humbert, if ever he thinks fit to assume possession of St. Peter's and the Vatican, should regard the erection of an Egyptian obelisk in the forecourt of a Renaissance church as a monstrous solecism in art, and so abolish one of the boldest and most impressive symbols ever devised to teach man that the "Lion of the Tribe of Judah" (with this title the obelisk is inscribed) "came out of Egypt," that the "great Serpent Pharaoh, King of Egypt" (or Nature) "is become Christ" by his assumption of the body which, without Him, is Egypt.

The Breviary, the Missal, the "Little Office," and other service books of the Church, are inexhaustible storehouses of such teaching, their leading method being the immediate apposition of passages from Scripture and the Fathers and prayers and ejaculations which, at first sight, have no related meaning, but in which the existence of a common meaning, which is the true one, is suggested, and may be discovered by those who have the key.

Besides the forms and offices of general use in the Church, there are, and have been, local rites, which it may have been, and may still be, expedient to suppress in favour of a wider uniformity; but of these there ought to be kept the most careful record. The dance before the altar, which still, I believe, is performed during Mass in some churches of Spain; the presentation, in other "local rites," to the officiating priest of the bread by a maiden and of the wine by a youth; and the like "customs" are all acted words of more or less significance, and are sometimes more interpretative of the Church's doctrine than any written speech.

Of course, the enlightened students of the magazines will laugh at the notion that there is any knowledge which can or ought, for their own sakes, to be concealed from them. I must content myself with the perhaps irrelevant remark that those who have hitherto been reputed the wisest have, in all ages, used and recommended such reticence, and would have understood and commended Aristotle when, in reply to Alexander's complaint that, in a certain book, the philosopher had published "secrets," he said: "They are published and not published, for none will learn from my book anything but that which he already knows." And I will add that neither in ancient nor in modern times has there been a poet, worthy of that sacred name, who would not have been horrified had he fancied that the full meaning of some of his sayings could be discerned by more than ten in ten thousand of his readers.

The denial by Mr. Grote and his followers that there is any parabolic or enigmatic meaning in the ancient mythologies is a most astounding proof of how men, of common sense in most things, will persistently deny, in the face of what ought to be absolutely convincing evidence to the contrary, that there may be anything to be understood in that which they cannot understand. It must be conceded, of course, that the teaching, if teaching be intended, in the Greek myths, is most unsystematic, and that the successive additions and modifications of the Homeric mythology, introduced by the Hesiodic and Orphic schools, brought in much confusion of names and attributes; but what is this against the presumption of a generally intelligent character in a mass of stories which, if it does not consist mainly of riddles, is as amazing, in its alternative character of incongruous nonsense, as the most enthusiastic neo-Platonist would have it to be in the character of a storehouse of psychological observation, a *Summa Theologiæ* of the great religion of which *Scire teipsum* was the first injunction, as it is, indeed, of Christianity. That Lord Bacon, and many others before and after him, should have given, as Taylor the Platonist says, "frigid and trifling interpretations" of the Greek myths, is surely no excuse to Mr. Grote and others for maintaining that a riddle, which is on the very face of it a riddle, has no answer.

On the other hand, what rational mind can see anything irrational in the belief that, to a race ardently believing in the Divine and in the capacity of man for Divine communications, every god and goddess represented a particular aspect of divinity towards the soul; and the soul, in each of its moods, activities, and capacities, some goddess or mistress of the gods; and that the adventures of gods, goddesses, nymphs, and heroes should often be parables of the phenomena of interior experience, experience too pure and subtle for common acquisition, and too sacred to be exposed to vulgar curiosity? And who are the best authorities upon the question, whether such significance was intended or not? Shall we follow Mr. Grote and the modern "scientists," with their "congenital incapacity" for spiritual realities, or Æschylus and a hundred others before him, who averred that these stories were life-giving mysteries, and the law-givers of their time who decreed the punishment of death against those who should explain them to the multitude?

The charge so often brought against the Church of having drawn upon these sources of illustration ought to constitute one of her highest claims to the admiration of a "liberal" age; for it amounts to this, that she alone has dared to recognise truth as canonical, wheresoever it may be discovered, and that she has not hesitated to appropriate the gold and silver vessels of her enemies, when they, of all others, were found fittest to contain the corresponding goods of spiritual perception and truths deducible from her faith. Nay, was not the Vine itself " brought out of Egypt," which, "when it had taken root, filled the land" of her former captives, and vivified with the inebriation of natural and intelligible hope the faith that would otherwise have been too spiritual for man? The Church does not dwell so often and emphatically on the coming of Christ "out of Egypt" for no reason. The designers of the first Cathedral of Christendom were not guilty of a ridiculous solecism when they placed an Egyptian obelisk at its entrance, or of utter vacuity of meaning when they inscribed it with the title, "The Lion of the Tribe of Judah."

IV

ATTENTION

ATTENTION to realities, rather than the fear of God, is "the beginning of wisdom"; but it seems to be the last effort of which the minds, even of cultivated people, are at present capable. No good and excellent thing requiring the least act of sustained attention to reality has any chance of recognition among us; original insight is dead, and men can see only the things which others, in less hasty times, have seen before them, and even these they can scarcely be said to see with their own eyes. Were the *Divine Comedy* to appear for the first time now, it would never be heard of, except in the small-type notices of the literary papers in which the young man who criticises poetry—because he has not learned to do anything else—would hasten to avail himself of so rare an opportunity of being funny. The faculty of attention to a line of scientific reasoning is common enough. It is the capacity for looking steadily at realities worthy of being reasoned about which is wanting. Through this impotence of attention, psychology has come to be a science the first axiom of which is that there is no soul, a denial which seems commonly to be owing, not so much to the vicious interest of corrupt passions, as to physical impatience of the attitude of attention demanded for the contemplation of human realities. Even the meats and wines of the epicure's table cannot be enjoyed without the habit of attention; hence the epicure's table is no more. Wealthy givers of dinners now trust, with scarcely any danger of discredit, to their guests' swallowing with applause whatever dainties are set before them, provided the consequent headache or colic is not immediately referable to its cause.

Much less will the nectar and ambrosia of the natural affections, for example, yield their flavours to the palate "studious to eat and not to taste." Through want of attention, more often, perhaps, than through inveterate vice, how many tread into the mud, with the foolish hoof of their lusts, the very flowers after which they are for ever in frantic search; and almost all men now bewail the impossibility of attaining the poor dolls which they dignify by the name of their "ideals," when Nature, "if we do but open and intend the eye," is always actually excelling every imagination of beauty; and realities, far lovelier than any "ideal," stand about us, willing to be wooed and longing to be won.

At least once in a lifetime, and by some hitherto unexplained awakening of full attention for a little while, what man but has seen a woman, and what woman a man, before whom all their previous "ideals" have paled; and if, by subsequent nearness, they get within the eyes' focus and the vision is dimmed, that is the fault of the eyes, and no discredit to the reality of the thing seen, as is proved by the way in which death restores the focus, and with it the vision. Attention, however, as multitudes have confessed with fruitless tears, would have adapted the focus of the eye to the nearness of the object, and made it more, not less, lovely by closer inspection.

Through inattention to their own true desires and capacities, men walk, as in a dream, among the trees of the Hesperides, hung with fruit the least savour of which includes the summed sweetness of all the flesh-pots of Egypt, yet so far surpasses it as, once tasted, to supersede for ever the lust of the eyes, the lust of the flesh, and the pride of life; but they do not dream of plucking them. The letter of Scripture is like the walls of a furnace, unsightly, and made of clay, but, to those who attend, full of chinks and crevices through which glows the white heat of a life whose mysteries of felicity it is "unlawful to utter"; but religious people are in too great a hurry of spirit to see anything but the clay walls, and they lead mean and miserable existences while loudly professing the faith which "hath the promise of this life also."

The hour or half-hour of daily "meditation," or attention to his own business, which used to be the practice of every good man, is now unheard of unless it be in Monasteries. The best among us, wholly unconscious that men can advance the world's improvement only by attending to their own, are busy about everything but that which concerns themselves, and after their dusty and profitless day's work they go, as Coleridge says, to the Divine Muses for *a*-musement. Hence, among many other unprecedented phenomena of our day, there is an almost complete lack of men of letters. We have only newspaper, magazine, and booksellers' hacks; clever enough, indeed, but without insight, character, or any care for, or desire to propagate, a knowledge of the true realities and delights of life.

Yet how vast are the rewards of a habit of attention, and how joyful an answer can the few who still practise it give to Wordsworth's question :—

> "Paradise and groves
> Elysian, Fortunate Fields—like those of old
> Sought in the Atlantic main—why should they be
> A history only of departed things,
> Or a mere fiction of what never was?
> For the discerning intellect of man,
> When wedded to this goodly universe
> In love and holy passion, shall find these
> A simple produce of the common day."

The habit, however, of such attention to realities as I am speaking of, is not to be formed without pain in those who have it not, unless they are possessed of mind and conscience, and something of the spirit of the child, that—

> "Mighty Prophet, Seer blest,
> On whom those truths do rest,
> Which we are toiling all our lives to find."

The soul which wants these qualifications, and has long dwelt easily and pleasantly and, perhaps, without external offence in unrealities, finds itself, when it endeavours to face reality, filled with an anguish of impatience, and rushes to and fro in the prison of its customs like a caged wild beast. There are thousands, however, who are not altogether so disqualified; and these, if they only looked, would "see in part and know in part" those eternal entities which, if not so seen and known now, will never be seen and known.

"Blessed," cries the Substantial Wisdom, "is he who explains me"; adding, in words of piercing but disregarded sweetness of invitation: "*Deliciæ meæ esse cum filiis hominum.*" With her, as with a mortal mistress, the one unpardonable crime is want of "attention."

It is not to be supposed, however, that the celestial secrets with which she rewards her steadfast votaries are to be attained, even by such as are naturally not disqualified, without considerable sacrifice of meaner goods. In the eyes of fools there is no such foolishness as the knowledge of things of which they know and can know nothing; and from such he who attends faithfully to his own true business will probably have much to suffer; for they will not be content with despising him for his infatuations, but they will hate him and do him what harm they can. He will also have to sequester himself from many natural and innocent interests and pleasures, in order to have time for the great learning, which is usually of slow acquisition, and the result of patient listening and of the hardly acquired habit of suspending *active thought*, which is the greatest of all enemies to *attention;* for "good thoughts are the free children of God, and do not come by thinking." He will also have to suffer from ordinarily good and well-intentioned people the charge of narrowness of benevolence as well as of intellect; for he will have no time or energy to spare for seeking out and serving other objects of charity, seeing that the knowledge of his own supreme needs will be increased by every day's addition to his immense but incommunicable treasure; incommunicable, indeed, now, but, as he learns from the Church, an addition to the everlasting treasure of all who are united with him in the "Body of Christ." Not that he will really be inoperative in the time being for good to others; for the mere life, however retired, of one in habitual communion with Wisdom, breathes forth a sphere of wisdom which extends far beyond its definable bounds; and, as for the "narrowness" with which he is charged, he may answer that the power of cleaving is in proportion to the narrowness of the edge and the weight at its back; and that the least of his words or actions may be of more effect in the world than the life's labour of any of the herd of good people who are "busied about much serving," instead of sitting attentive at the feet of Truth.

V

CHRISTIANITY AN EXPERIMENTAL SCIENCE

CHRISTIANITY is an experimental science, and the best answer to one who questions, If it be true, is, Try it. But one difference between this and other experimental sciences is, that the necessary course of experiment is almost always, in the beginning at least, extremely difficult, painful, and repugnant to nature. Another is, that the result, though, provided this course be conducted with full sincerity and patience, sure to be absolutely convincing to the experimentalist, will not be wholly communicable or convincing to anybody else. It will give, indeed, to the person who has attained it, certain characteristics of manner, speech, and action which will strongly tend to impress any honest man that the experiment may be worth trying on his own behalf; but that is all.

The experiments and conclusions of the natural

sciences can be discerned and judged by the natural senses, which all men have in common, and which have no interest in being blind to the facts of nature. But the spiritual senses, except in the exceedingly rare cases of some men of genius, in whom they appear to exist independently of the moral perfection which is their commonly indispensable condition, have scarcely any life in the great mass of men, who live, often virtuously, or at least decorously, contented with knowing and enjoying only in their natural shadows those realities which are devoutly and substantially discerned by that higher order of perception which is usually the ultimate reward of so "doing God's commandments" that we may "know of the doctrine."

The multitude, Catholic and otherwise, who are, as Sir Thomas Browne says, "incapable of perfectness," have branded this science with the name of "mysticism." Cardinal Wiseman, accepting the name, defines "mysticism" as being "the science of love." What wonder if experimental knowledge in this science should be scarcely at all accessible to the vast majority of souls, in whom the seed of love has never yet passed beyond its rudimentary and apparently opposite state of fear, and who really regard the very notion of personal love to God and delight in communion with Him as a sort of irreverence,—which, in them, indeed, it would be! There is, in fact, no Church but one which, as a rule, ventures even to propose this kind of love as the end and crown of its teaching. St. Evremond says that the most characteristic difference between that Church and all others is that, while the one makes it the ambition of the soul to please Him, the others seek only to avoid displeasing Him; love being the principle in the one case, fear in the other. The "science of love" is, indeed, "mysticism" to the many who fancy its experiences—incommunicable as the odour of a violet to those who have never smelt one—to be those of idiosyncratical enthusiasm or infatuation; but, among "mystics" themselves, the terms of this science are common property. Deep calleth unto deep a prophecy which is not of "private interpretation," but one which has a language as clear as is that of the sciences of the dust, and as strict a consensus of orthodoxy. A St. Catherine of Genoa and a St. John of the Cross know each what the other is saying, though, to a Huxley or a Morley, it is but a hooting of owls.

There are infinite degrees of this experimental knowledge, from that first sensible "touch" of God's love, which usually accompanies the first sincere intention of perfection for His sake, to that of the Saints who have united themselves to God by a series of agonising initiations of self-sacrifice, and by years of actual and habitual perfection of obedience in the smallest as well as the greatest things; and, further still, to the knowledge of the angels, whose purification and consequent capacity goes on increasing for ever. But the very first sincere experiment, and its perceptible result, though they may be followed by years and years of relapse and seeming failure, are generally final. The man who has made the experiment has seen God; and that is an event which he will never be able altogether to forget or deny, a positive fact which, for reality and self-evidence, stands alone in his experience, and which no amount of negative evidence will be able, even for a moment, to obscure.

For this first experiment of faith, a belief in a personal God and in His right to command and judge us, is the only dogmatic ground which is required, and this ground almost every form of religion affords; and that "touch" of love which, as the Church says, "supersedes all the sacraments," is given to each one, who, with all his heart, even for an hour, submits himself to the guidance of the "Light which lighteth every man who cometh into the world." If his memory clings, with however poor a fidelity, to that first kiss of God, that baptism of fire which is the tacit knowledge of the Incarnation—for is it not God made one with his body, *i.e.* his senses?—that initiating perception that God *is* will lead him into further actual illumination in proportion to his fidelity and to the amount of Catholic dogma which his particular Church may be capable of teaching—for fidelity does not *discover* dogma, but only enables the faithful, in proportion to their faith, to confirm it with absolute personal assurance. *False* dogmas cannot be believed with this experimental certainty because they do not represent realities; therefore such dogmas will not be believed by any one who has seen God, in such a way as finally to hinder the saving power of the true teaching. Thus, in Churches and sects which teach dogmas in themselves subversive of all morality and right belief in God's nature and government, we find individuals so deeply rooted in the fundamental orthodoxy of love, that, while daily professing with their mouths the immoral and pernicious doctrines of their sect, they so deny these doctrines in their hearts and lives, that the only harm—a very great one indeed—which befalls them from this position, is the impossibility of adequately developing their own nature. Each great Catholic dogma is the key, and the only key, to some great mystery, or series of mysteries, in humanity; and, this dogma wanting, the humanity of the individual is so far deprived of the means of eternal development; which must be initiated in this life, if at all. But, in any case, provided he has attained "to lay his just hand on that golden key which opes the palace of eternity," by absolute fidelity to his best light, the *truths*, which he has adopted by faith, become "*res visa et cognita*," in a sense of which Lord Bacon did not dream; for Lord Bacon's "philosophy," as philosophy, was even baser than his political career, and it did not deal with "things," which are the objects of Wisdom, but with phenomena, which are only hints and corroborations of realities discovered by that which is philosophy indeed.

A duck-pond, however, must not be expected to grow salmon or pike, and the offspring of the conventicle will always remain narrow in the possibilities of experimental knowledge as compared with those who have been fed in the larger waters which occasionally bring forth a Hooker or a Keble, as again these are when compared with the ocean-brood of Austins, Bernards, and Theresas.

But, wherever the elementary dogmas of Christianity are taught, there the man who is *perfectly* sincere and faithful is in the possibility of an infinitely precious experimental knowledge; and that knowledge, however limited (and the knowledge even of the angels is limited), will fit him for his destined place in the communion of Saints, and may raise him far higher in God's favour than other Saints who may have discerned and loved a wider truth, truly, indeed, but with less intensity. Such men are Christ's beloved "poor" (not the world's "poor," who are quite as proud, vicious, luxurious, and covetous of this world's goods as the world's "rich"), and, though they have been fed only with crumbs from the table of those who sit at feasts of the fullest orthodoxy, such crumbs will nourish in them a life which the merely "wise and learned" in the letter of divine truth can never know.

To such a man the Incarnation becomes, not the central dogma of his faith, but the central fact of his experience; for it is going on perceptibly in himself; the Trinity becomes the only and self-evident explanation of mysteries which are daily wrought in his own complex nature, the result of the *fiat*: "Let us make man in our own image;' and he finds in his soul and body the answer to the prayer, "Let me so behold Thy presence in righteousness, that I may wake up after Thy likeness and be satisfied with it." Like Teiresias, he has seen the unveiled wisdom, and thenceforth can see nothing else; his guide is thenceforward, not formal laws or truths which can be uttered, but the golden rod of a supreme good, which leads him infallibly (and most sensibly) by glowing into greater felicity so long as he is in the right path, and by fading, more or less, as he is in danger of error. Like Teiresias, again, on the mountain heights of contemplation persevered in through years and years, he strikes, from time to time, with his golden staff upon interwoven mysteries of nature, and finds in them the revelation of undreamt-of secrets of his own being; and he finally becomes, not so much an adorer as an actual participator in the nature and felicity of that Divinity which alone " has fruition in Himself," and "who became man that men might become gods."

VI

"A PEOPLE OF A STAMMERING TONGUE"

IN things of the spirit we can only "know in part and see in part" and "as in a glass darkly." Hence, in writing concerning these things, the aphoristic manner always has been and always will be found the most proper and fructifying. In spiritual philosophy the blessing of systematic perfection has ever been paid for by the curse of barrenness; for between the facts of the science of the soul there is often no visible continuity and sometimes an appearance of contradiction; and in such cases we have to be contented with the simple perception and affirmation that they *are*. Again, such facts, in proportion to their importance, are simple and self-evident; and, in proportion to their simplicity and self-evidence, they are, as Aristotle says, apart from the domain of the reasoning faculty, and therefore unintelligible and incredible to those who have acquired the habit of relying, not upon reason, but upon reasoning, for proof. Nothing can be more express than the way in which this is over and over again asserted and implied by Our Lord and His Apostles. "None can say that Jesus is the Lord but by the Holy Ghost," that is, by the spirit of direct vision. "I tell you these things, not because ye know them not, but because ye know them." "The Holy Ghost shall *teach* you whatsoever I shall have *said* unto you," etc.

Dogmatic truth is the key and the soul of man is the lock; the proof of the key is in its opening of the lock; and, if it does that, all other evidence of its authenticity is superfluous, and all attempts to disprove it are absurd in the eyes of a sensible person. That only a very small proportion of the human race should be capable of at once receiving self-evident truth is quite natural. The key is not less the key because it will not open a lock of which the wards are filled with stones and rusted by disuse or destroyed by sin. "Authority" comes in here. When a man "speaking with authority," that is, with the indescribable air and character which is an unmistakable claim to being listened to, affirms things beyond all ordinary experience and credibility, and adds that it is only by "doing the commandments" that we can "know of the doctrine," a sincere and businesslike mind will at least consider the experiment of that moral perfection, to which such wonderful things are promised, worth trying ; and, if he tries with full integrity of purpose and persistence, all persons who have reached that perfection assure us that he will not fail to attain to that direct vision to which truths, received on "authority" as "dogmas," gradually become discernible as *facts*, "infinitely visible and credible" (as St. Augustine says of God) and of incomparable personal interest to himself. The infinite visibility and credibility of such facts imply a counterpart of infinite invisibility and incredibility. "The angels themselves desire to look into these things" and to fathom them fully, but in vain. The higher they soar in the light of vision the more manifestly incomplete and "unsystematic" is their theology ; and their knowledge becomes more and more merely and absolutely "nuptial knowledge," that is, the knowledge of fruition, for which there is no intelligible word nor "reason."

When the soul has passed the "purgative" stage of obedience to law, and has attained the "unitive" condition, in which all fidelity is habitual and comparatively easy, she becomes capable, for the first time, of real "insight," and knowledge ceases to be acceptance of "dogma" so much as personal communion. She exclaims, "The Lord hath fashioned me and laid his hand upon me"; but she adds, "Such knowledge is too excellent for me; I cannot attain unto it"; and the utterances whereby she endeavours to draw others to her wisdom are interjections, doxologies, parables, and aphorisms, which have no connecting unity but that of a common heat and light.

Another reason for the inadequacy of expression in the science of the soul is the "unlawfulness" of speech concerning some of its most essential facts. St. Paul, in his vision, says he saw things which it was, not impossible, but "unlawful" to utter. Again, the spectators of the Transfiguration were commanded not to tell the Vision to any man until Christ should be risen, that is, until Christ should be risen in their auditor, it being lawful to speak of the mysteries revealed in that Vision only to those who already know. Again, the Bridegroom of the soul loves to reserve to Himself the office of her instructor in His secrets; and the more she has learned the less will she be willing to speak. "My secret to me," is the reply of the Saints to inquirers concerning their peculiar knowledge. "Night," says the Soul, "is the light of my pleasures," and she refuses by speech to obscure them with the darkness of day. Furthermore, her confession of such knowledge involves incurring the praise of man for having corresponded with peculiar fidelity to the graces of God; and she abhors the praises of any but Him, whose assurance that He "greatly desires her beauty" makes all lesser laudation profane and disgusting.

Besides the pride and modesty of the pure soul, there is yet another reason why those who know most speak least. There comes a time to those who follow perfection, in which all possible forms of beauty are, as it were, discerned at once; it is not beautiful things, but Beauty itself which is perceived; and in the light of this faint aurora of the great and unspeakable vision, all particular forms of beauty, such as quicken the tongue of Art, fail to arrest interest and attention and to excite the desire of communicating them to others. A sculptor who could see, at one moment, all the possible forms of beauty which might be wrought from his block of marble would be quite unanxious and unable to develop any one of them.

VII

THE BOW SET IN THE CLOUD

IT may be a matter of surprise to many that I, professing to be an orthodox Christian, should frequently use language which seems to assume that some knowledge of Christian mysteries has been enjoyed by individuals in all times and places; that the light which lighteth every man who cometh into the world shone, more or less obscurely, before the days of Him who came to bring light into the world.; but this is a belief and a conviction which is growing more and more general with the growing light which the contemplations of Saints and Doctors have cast upon Catholic doctrine; and it need present no great difficulty to the mind, however scrupulous to keep within safe limits of faith, if it be borne in remembrance that the Incarnation was an act done in eternity as well as time; that the Lamb, the "I am before Abraham was," was "slain from the beginning"; and that, if we look from the point of view of eternity, we may see that effects of that act, apparently retrospective, were not really so; but that the Bread and Wine, without which "there is no life in us," may have been received from the hand of an invisible Melchisedech by many who, in time, have longed to see the Day of the Lord, and have done their best, by heroic purity and self-humiliation, to merit the Vision, and have thus attained to that love which, as St. Augustine says, "supersedes all the sacraments."

Nor do glimpses of the heavenly vision seem to have been absolutely denied to any race of men. The general "darkness that comprehendeth it not" seems occasionally to have been lifted among races whose night is by most good people presumed to be total. The religious rites of "savage" nations sometimes startle those who know the meaning of the rites of the Church by a strange identity of significance. God's mercy is over all His works, and He does not refuse to such babes and sucklings some effectual hints of that knowledge which is especially promised to babes and sucklings, and denied to the wise and learned. Finally, let me note that the anthropomorphic character, which so universally marks the religion of the simple and is so great a scandal to the "wise," may be regarded as a remote confession of the Incarnation, a saving instinct of the fact that a God who is not a man is, for man, no God.

The mystery of triple Personality in one Being, the acknowledgment of which is the prime condition of a real apprehension of God, may be best approached by the human mind under the analogue of difference of sex in one entity; as it was by Plato and by much earlier Greek Philosophers, and, more or less obscurely, by the " wise ancients" of India and Egypt, and, for the first time, quite clearly shadowed forth by the Scriptures and the Church; Nature herself adding her crowning witness, without which men are incapable of effectually grasping any spiritual truths. "In the beginning" (*i.e.* before men had lost their original knowledge of God and His Image in Man) "there were," says Plato, "three sexes." The saying, "God is a beautiful Youth and a Divine nymph" is attributed to Orpheus. By the Church the Second Person is represented as the "glory" of the "Father," who is Christ's "Head," as Man is the glory of his Head, Christ, and Woman the glory of Man, who is her head. The individual Man, the *homo*, is the Image of God in so far as he is a substantial reflection of the Love, the Truth, and the Life, which last is the "embrace" of Truth and Love, as the Holy Spirit is said by the Church to be the "embrace" of the First Person and the Second. And nature goes on giving echoes of the same living triplicity in animal, plant, and mineral, every stone and material atom owing its being to the synthesis or "embrace" of the two opposed forces of expansion and contraction. Nothing whatever exists in a single entity but in virtue of its being thesis, antithesis, and synthesis, and in humanity and natural life this takes the form of sex, the masculine, the feminine, and the neuter, or third, forgotten sex spoken of by Plato, which is not the absence of the life of sex, but its fulfilment and power, as the electric fire is the fulfilment and power of positive and negative in their "embrace."

Man (*homo*), according to the writer of Genesis, originally contained the woman, and was in his individual self the synthesis; and the separation into distinct bodies has been regarded by some theologians as a consequence of the fall, from which the regenerated will recover in that state in which there is no giving or receiving in marriage, man (*homo*) himself *being* a marriage and "as the angels in heaven,"—a change which is already foreshadowed in the "Brides of Christ" by that which is their most sensible characteristic, namely, a marked increase of the feminine nature, which is passive, humble, receptive, sensitive, and responsive; this increase, however, so far from being at the expense of the masculine character, that this latter is exalted into fuller strength, invincible courage, and greater wisdom to command all that is below him, especially his own feminine nature—whose rebellions, in his natural condition, are the cause of all his disasters.

"Receive thy glory" (womanhood "the glory of the man") "with joy," says St. Paul to those who had newly seen the unveiled wisdom; and, in the wonderful parable of Teiresias, that change or rather discovery in his own nature was the first effect of the same vision, which blinded him, as it does any one who has beheld it, to all other objects of sight. This three-coloured Iris (the "Messenger of Juno," the Divine womanhood), is also the "Bow set in the cloud" of the renewed nature, for a promise that it shall never again be overwhelmed and destroyed by the deluge of the disordered senses.

According to Christian theology, it was the Second Person, the "glory" of God the Father, who took on actual womanhood or "body" in the body of the Blessed Virgin, and who imparts the same to all who partake of the same body in the Holy Sacrament; and accordingly it is said by St. Augustine, that "Christ is the Bride as well as the Bridegroom, for He is the Body"; and St. John of the Cross says that, in the last heights of contemplation, man attains to contemplate Him as the Bride, an attainment corresponding to the second change of Teiresias after his seven years of meditation on the first.

VIII

CHRISTIANITY AND "PROGRESS"

MANY people doubt whether Christianity has done much, or even anything, for the "progress" of the human race as a race; and there is more to be said in defence of such doubt than most good people suppose. Indeed, the expression of this doubt is very widely regarded as shocking and irreligious, and as condemnatory of Christianity altogether. It is considered to be equivalent to an assertion that Christianity has hitherto proved a "failure." But some who do not consider that Christianity has proved a failure, do, nevertheless, hold that it is open to question whether the race, as a race, has been much affected by it, and whether the external and visible evil and good which have come of it do not pretty nearly balance one another.

As to the question of the real failure or success of Christianity, that must be settled by considering the purpose of its Founder. Did He come into the world, live and die for "the greatest happiness of the greatest number," as that is commonly understood, and as it constitutes the end of civil government? Was it His main purpose, or any part of His purpose, that everybody should have plenty to eat and drink, comfortable houses, and not too much to do? If so, Communism must be allowed to have more to say for itself, on religious grounds, than most good Christians would like to admit. Did He expect or prophesy any great and general amelioration of the world, material or even moral, from His coming? If not, then it cannot be said that Christianity has failed because these and other like things have not come of it. In these days all truth is shocking; and it is to be feared that the majority of good people may feel shocked by the denial, even in His own words, that such ends had anything more than an accidental part in His purpose or expectation. He and His Apostles did not prophesy that the world would get better and happier for His life, death, and teaching; but rather that it would become intolerably worse. He foretells that the world will continue to persecute such as dare to be greatly good, and that it will consider that it does God service in killing them. He tells us that the poor will be always with us, and does not hint disapproval of the institution even of slavery, though He counsels the slave to be content with his status. His mission is most clearly declared to be wholly individual and wholly unconcerned with the temporal good of the individual, except in so far as "faith hath the promise of this life also"; and moreover, what is yet more "shocking" to modern sensibilities, He very clearly declared that, though He lived and died to give all a chance, the number of individuals to be actually benefited by His having done so would be few; so that it was practically for these few only that He lived and died. That may be very shocking; but they are *His* words, and not mine, and those who do not like them should have a special edition of the New Testament revised for their own use, from which all disagreeable references to the many called and few chosen, the narrow way which few find, the broad road generally taken, and the end it leads to, etc., etc., should be excised. It is not to be denied that our Lord's doctrine must be in the highest degree unpleasant to all who will consider what it really is, and who have not the courage either to reject it or adopt it in a whole-hearted manner.

But has Christianity failed in doing that which alone it professed to do? It has not improved and has not professed to improve bad or even indifferently good people who form the mass of mankind, but it does profess to do great things when it is received in "a good and honest heart," that is, in the heart—according to Hamlet's estimate—of about one in ten thousand. The question, then, of failure or success narrows itself to this: Has Christianity done great things, infinitely great things; and has it all along been doing, and is it now doing, such things, for the very small proportion of mankind with which it professes to be effectually concerned? Professor Huxley says frankly, No. It emasculates and vitiates human character; and he exemplifies his position by the example of the Saints of the order of St. Francis. It is well to have such a good, bold statement of opinion. Here is no shilly-shallying, and we now know that there are some persons, of strong common sense, who think that Christianity *is* a failure, as having failed to carry out its professions. Few persons who are in their right wits would choose to seek a fencing-match with Professor Huxley. They might be altogether in the right, and yet, as Sir Thomas Browne says, they might come off second best in the conflict. In any case, it is not at present my affair. It is enough for me to point out that it is conceivable that there are sciences, even "experimental" sciences, in which Professor Huxley has not yet qualified himself to be considered as an expert. Christianity professes to be such a science, a strictly experimental science, only differing, in this character, from chemistry, inasmuch as the experiments and their conditions can, in the one case, be easily fulfilled and judged by the senses which are common to all men; whereas, in the other, they are *professedly* to be fulfilled and judged of by few. Here, again, come in those unpleasant assertions of the founders of Christianity: " None can say that Jesus is the Lord but by the Holy Ghost"; "Do my commandments and ye shall know of the doctrine," etc., etc.—*i.e.* the experiment is *professedly* to be made only with great difficulty and self-denial, and its results can be judged solely by a spirit or sense which is only attainable, or which is, at least, only attained, by a few.

The conclusion is this, then, that even if Christianity—as I do not assert—has not sensibly affected "progress," or has affected it as much for the worse in some directions as for the better in others, and has not even done much individual good in more than a very small proportion even of those who call themselves Christians, it has only not done what it never professed to do. But has it done what it actually professed to do? That is a question of which the affirmative might be difficult of absolute and generally intelligible *proof*, but of which the negative must, I apprehend, be considered absurd even by the great majority of those who have never dreamed of qualifying themselves to become final judges of such matters.

There are many passages in Scripture which will readily occur to every reader as being on the surface in contradiction to this limitation by our Lord's own words of the primary purpose of Christianity; but those who know how orphaned and widowed of truth even the best of us are, and how the destitution we may discover in ourselves is greater than that we can know of in any others, will discern, with the earlier and deeper interpreters of the words of our Lord and His Apostles, that there are two ways of reading their exhortations to help the poor and the declaration that to visit the orphan and the widow is "pure religion and undefiled"; and they will understand that neighbourly service, which is usually (but not always) an inseparable accidental duty of Christian life, is very far indeed from being of primary consequence, though the rendering or not rendering of it—where there is no knowledge of a nobler service—may seriously affect the shallow heavens and the shallow hells of the feebly good and the feebly wicked. Let not such as these exalt themselves against the great Masters of the experimental science of Life, one of whom—St. Theresa, if I remember rightly

—declares that more good is done by one minute of reciprocal contemplative communion of love with God than by the founding of fifty hospitals or of fifty churches. "The elect soul," says another great experimentalist, St. Francis of Sales, "is a beautiful and beloved lady, of whom God demands not the indignity of service, but desires only her society and her person."

IX

SIMPLICITY

THERE are three simplicities; that of the child, "On whom those truths do rest which we are toiling all our lives to find"; the simplicity of genius; and the simplicity of wisdom. "The single eye, which makes the body full of light"—in modern phrase, the synthetical faculty and habit—is the essential character of all simplicity, and it is never separated from a certain innocence and *naïveté;* and quiescence or perfection of conscience appear to be its conditions. The paradisaical, or synthetic, vision in the child is conditioned by the innocence of ignorance and its inevitable freedom from the habit of analysis; the mind of the child goes forth into particulars with a congenital discernment of the living unity of which the child itself is, as yet, a part; and it continues so to go forth until it falls into some disorder of will or understanding or both, which is separation from that unity, and extinction of "the single eye." Genius consists wholly in the possession of the divine faculty of synthetic or unitive apprehension, in maturer years, and in company with consciousness or the power of reflection. This possession is so exceedingly rare, whole nations and generations having existed without producing a single noticeable instance of it, that it must be regarded, not as the natural culmination of humanity, but as a splendid and fortunate anomaly, or departure from the law of the race. In some few of the very few, indeed, it seems to have been in natural order, the simplicity and purity of childhood having been retained and developed through life, until it has become the simplicity of wisdom; but no one who has made himself acquainted with the lives of men of genius can fail to have observed that a concomitant of their wonderful privilege has usually been a certain dislocation and startling disproportion in faculty and character. Simplicity or *naïveté*, as Lessing remarks, has invariably more or less characterised them and their work; but, in most instances they seem, if one may say so, to have had no moral right to this singular grace, and even sometimes to have preserved or attained it by bold denial or by mere oblivion of its natural conditions—an oblivion not unfrequently amounting to moral insanity. It has, in such cases, been like the precious gum, or profuse flush of flower, which comes of disease in the tree. The three constituent parts of man, the intellect, will, and perception, in such cases, do not act together, as they do in healthy persons, but the exorbitancy of perception seems to be the result of a lethargy of intellect and will which leaves the whole energy of life to go forth into perception, as it does in the child through like conditions, conditions which in the child, however, are the right order of its being. The past century, which has been so extraordinarily productive of men of genius, has produced a more than usual proportion of those in whom genius has been the concomitant of mental and moral defect and disorder. The works of such men are marked by exceeding inequality, deserts of dulness as in Coleridge, or of mere imbecility as in Blake, occasionally and suddenly blossoming as the rose, or the intermittent flush of beauty and fictitious health in the face of one dying of decline.

There is another kind of simplicity, which is endowed, like the others, with the synthetic eye, and which is the only kind that is of much abiding value to its possessor; namely, the simplicity of wisdom. This is rarely found except in persons of advanced years. The simplicity of age is the blossom of which that of childhood is the bud and almost always failing promise. Its great condition is innocence, which has been retained through, or recovered during, the struggles and temptations of manhood; and, as the innocence of knowledge is far nobler than that of infantine ignorance, so its reward, the unitive vision, has an immeasurably wider field. Such men, at seventy, see again the daisy as they saw it when they were seven; but a universe of realities, unknown in childhood, is discerned by them as a single flower of which each particular reality is a petal; and the life-long unconscious analysis, which has been to other men corruption, has only provided them with a vaster prospect of the elemental integrity, and an inexhaustible source of joy, which, like that of the "young-eyed cherubim," is too grave for smiles.

X
ANCIENT AND MODERN IDEAS OF PURITY

FEW persons who are not scholars have any knowledge of the difference which there is between ancient and modern ideas of purity, and few moralists have considered or admitted how very largely the comparison, if fairly made, must tell in favour of the ancients, who may be reckoned, in this matter, to have ceased about the time of the Reformation. As it was impurity which first. brought fig-leaves into fashion, so the wonderful and altogether unprecedented addiction to that fashion, during the past three hundred years, may be taken as a fair measure of what puritanism has done, during that period, for us, and is still doing, —still doing, for, within the last few years, the actual fig-leaf has invaded the Vatican itself; and even there we are no longer allowed to contemplate "the human form divine," unprofaned by reminders of the niceness of nasty thinkers.

If we go back to those first ages of Christianity—which modern good people, who know nothing about them, regard with such reverence—we shall find that the greatest and purest of the "Fathers of the Church" were in the practice of addressing their flocks with an outspokenness which is not surpassed even by the ancient expounders of the Eleusinian and Bacchic mysteries, or, for that matter, by the Bible itself. St. Augustine, for example, in the *City of God* and elsewhere, says things fit to throw decent people into convulsions; and nowhere, in ancient Christian writings, do we find ignorance regarded as even a part, much less the whole, of innocence :—witness the words of Her, who is the model of innocence to all ages, in her answer, at thirteen years of age, to the message of Gabriel.

Strange to say, this modern notion of purity is not limited to those Churches which owe their origin to the Reformation. Their spirit has so deeply infected the Mother Church that, though her abstract doctrine remains the same as it was, she practically enforces the negative idea as jealously as it is enforced among good Protestants, or even more jealously, so that the ancient idea of positive purity, as a sacred fire which consumes and turns into its own substance all that is adverse to it, is now replaced by the conception that it is of the nature of stored snow, which must be kept artificially dark and cool, lest it disappear for ever. "Why, papa, I thought that marriage was rather a wicked sacrament!" said a young lady, who had been brought up at one of the best convent schools in England, the other day to her father, when he happened to be praising that institution. And in the great English Catholic Colleges for boys, the wonderful phenomenon may now be seen of two or three hundred lads and young men whose minds, with regard to the relations of the sexes, are exactly in the same condition as those of the girls, and whose only idea of marriage—gathered from the shyness with which the whole subject is avoided by all about them—is, that it is "rather a wicked sacrament." The prolongation of the innocence of ignorance into advanced youth would probably be unmixed gain were it not that knowledge, being left to come by accident, is almost sure to become poisoned in the moment of acquisition. It is of little use calling the legitimate connexion of the sexes a "great sacrament," if no pains are taken to identify the knowledge of that connexion with the knowledge of what is meant by a sacrament, this latter knowledge being the ground of the immense difference between the pagan and Christian views of marriage, and if the essential sanctity of chastity, married or unmarried, is left to be discovered only by the obscuration of the conscience in its loss. The whole sphere of the doctrines of the early Church, like that of all the great mythologies, revolved about mysteries which the modern Churches, in practice, absolutely ignore, but which nature, however improved by grace, absolutely refuses to ignore. The result is a practical Manicheism, which is as serious in its effects upon morals as it is treasonous to the truth. The prodigious evils of unchastity prove sufficiently that chastity is no merely negative good. *Corruptio optimi pessima.* But where is the safeguard of purity if its corruption is imagined to be the corruption, not of the "best," but of some shadowy and negative state? To avoid this immeasurable evil there should be prudent and bold plain-speaking on fitting occasions.

Plain-speaking does not vitiate. Even coarseness is health compared with those suppressed forms of the disease of impurity which come of our modern undivine silences.

A young man or woman must be hopelessly corrupt who would be injured by the freest reading of the Bible, or Shakespeare. The most pure and exalted love-poem that was ever written, Spenser's *Epithalamion* on his own marriage, is also one of the most "nude"; and all art-students "from the life" know that it is ingenious dress far more than the absence of dress that has dangerous attractions.

The boldest confession of the doctrine of the Incarnation, with all its corollaries, has been the father of that splendid virtue which was but dimly foreshown in pre-Christian ideas of purity. Wherever this doctrine has been denied or hesitatingly taught, it is a fact of simple experience that chastity has suffered with it. For what considerations can ordinary morals or the widest suggestions of worldly expediency substitute for those with which the New Testament abounds? "Bear and glorify God in your bodies"; "Shall I take the members of Christ and make them the members of a harlot?" "God for the body, and the body for God," etc.

XI

CONSCIENCE

THE twofold constitution of man which, the more it is reflécted upon, becomes the more manifest and wonderful, and seems more and more to approach the reality of a double personality in one being—the duality which the old theologians and philosophers recognised in speaking of man's nature as composed of a rational and of a sensitive, or of a male and female soul—is in nothing more obvious to persons who really consider their own business than in the phenomena of conscience. In every person who has a right to be called a person, as distinguished from an animal, there are two distinct consciences: the rational or male conscience, that commands him to act according to certain fixed laws which he knows or believes to be just and right; and the sensitive or female conscience, which persuades, indeed, to apparent good, but which, in default of habitual subordination to the virile conscience, does more harm in the world, although it is a sort of virtue, than is done by any vice. It is full of scruples about small things, and is often indifferent to great. Its chief care is for things present and external. To sympathise with and alleviate present and physical or emotional suffering and evils often simply fanciful, and to forgive things which ought not to be forgiven, is the extent of its "charity"; and its character, in all but highly disciplined and robust minds, is to be in almost continual conflict with the rational conscience. So that the struggles of a really good man are not so much against evil, which, known to be such, does not attract him, as against the inexpedient good which his inferior conscience is perpetually recommending to him with the most confusing plausibility, and which, if it be not listened to, cries out against him with lamentations and reproaches, often hard to distinguish from the voice of his own proper guide. It is so especially when, as is mostly the case, this female objurgator charges him with refusing to make sacrifices which are not only uncalled for, but would be injurious to his own true welfare and that of others, if they were made. This conflict caused the Apostle to cry out, "The whole creation groaneth together until now, waiting for the manifestation of the sons of God, to wit the redemption of the body"—the "body," the "woman," and the sensitive "soul" being synonyms to his mind as to that of all ancient philosophers. The sons of God—*i.e.* the true and faithful—however perfect in will and deed, cannot be "manifested" while they are thus in opposition to their sensitive life, which should be their helpmate and "glory" instead of their troublesome adversary and accuser. In some exceedingly small proportion of good people this glowing female conscience has been so persistently resisted and ordered by severe and undeviating obedience to "cold" and purely rational dictates, that such persons are not only no longer troubled by the insubordination and contradictions of the sensitive nature, but they find themselves—often suddenly and unexpectedly —in more or less complete harmony and co-operation with her. She has submitted; and the true life, which had been hitherto arduous and full of trouble, is thenceforward full of the joy as well as the power of the Divine Spirit, she having become his "glory," as she was before his accuser and shame, and the means instead of the hinderer of his "manifestation" as a "son of God."

It must be repeated, however, that the inferior conscience is not a vice, but a virtue without sufficient light; and that it is far more likely to call for unnecessary labour and sacrifice and to suggest false and harassing scruples than to invite to ease and self-indulgence. The *false* conscience, by which the mass of men justify to themselves their persistence in ignorance and self-seeking, or brace themselves to the difficult pursuit of unjust ends without regard to law, is a very different thing.

It should be remembered that even the truest conscience is not an illuminating power, though illumination is sure to follow obedience to it. It is a commanding voice, that bids all and compels some to follow their best attainable light ; which being done, there is no sin, though there may be great and temporarily terrible error in such obedience. So much for the individual conscience. Let it be added that when a whole nation comes to be mainly guided by the female or sensitive conscience, so far as it has any conscience at all, then great disaster is not far off.

XII

REAL APPREHENSION

"MAN," says Dr. Newman, "is not a reasoning animal; he is a seeing, feeling, contemplating, acting animal." To see rightly is the first of human qualities; right feeling and right acting are usually its consequences. There are two ways of seeing: one is to comprehend, which is to see all round a thing, or to embrace it; one is to apprehend, which is to see it in part, or to take hold of it. A thing may be really taken hold of which is much too big for embracing. Real apprehension implies reality in that which is apprehended. You cannot "take hold" of that which is nothing. The notional grasp which some people seen to have of clouds and mares' nests is a totally different thing from real apprehension; though what this difference is could scarcely be made clear to those who have no experience of the latter. A man may not be able to convey to another his real apprehension of a thing; but there will be something in his general character and way of discoursing which will convince you, if you too are a man acquainted with realities, that he has truly got hold of what he professes to have got hold of, and you will be wary of denying what he affirms. The man of real apprehensions, or the truly sensible man, has no opinions. Many things may be dubious to him; but if he is compelled to act without knowledge, he does so promptly, being prompt to discern which of the doubtful ways before him is the least questionable, on the ground of such evidence as he has. As to what he sees to be true or right, he does not argue with the person who differs from him upon a vital point, but only avoids his company, or, if he be of an irascible temperament, feels inclined to knock him down. Of course there are some people who see things which do not exist; but this is lunacy, and beyond the scope of these remarks. Real apprehension is emphatically the quality which constitutes "good sense." Common good sense has a real apprehension of innumerable things which those who add to good sense learning and reflection may comprehend; but there is much that must for ever remain matter only of real apprehension to the best seers; that is to say, everything in which the infinite has a part, *i.e.* all religion, all virtue as distinguished from temporary expediency, the grounds of all true art, etc. A man may have an immense acquaintance with facts; he may have all history and the whole circle of the sciences on the tip of his tongue; he may be the author of a classical system of logic, or may have so cunningly elaborated a false theory of nature as to puzzle and infuriate the wisest of men: and yet may not really apprehend any part of the truth of life which is properly human knowledge. At the present time it is by politics chiefly that the difference between the two great classes of men is made apparent. For the first time in English history, party limitations coincide almost exactly with the limitations which separate silly from sensible men. If you talk with a sincere Gladstonian— and, wonderful to say, there are still many such— you will soon find that he has no real apprehension of anything. He only feebly and foolishly opines.

It is not to be concluded from what has been said that the possession of the apprehending faculty in any way supersedes the good of learning. The power of really apprehending is nothing in the absence of realities to be apprehended. In the great field of ordinary social relationships and duties the subject-matter of such apprehension is largely supplied by individual experience, and the exercise by most men of that faculty is in the main limited to these; so that the praise of "good sense" has acquired a much narrower signification than it ought to bear. Genius is nothing but great good sense, or real apprehension, exercised upon objects more or less out of common sight: and the chief ingredient of even the highest and most heroic sanctity is the same apprehension taking hold upon spiritual truths and applying them to the conduct of the interior as well as the exterior life. Men with great strength of real apprehension are easily capable of things which inferior characters regard as great self-sacrifices. To such men such things are no more sacrifice than in an ordinary man it would be to exchange a ton of lead for a pound of gold. "Their hearts do not forget the things their eyes have seen;" and persons like General Gordon or Sir Thomas More would stare if you called anything they did or suffered by the name of sacrifice.

You cannot read the writings of Newman, Hooker, Pascal and St. Augustine, without being strongly impressed with the presumption that they have a real apprehension of the things they profess to believe; and, since they do not justify in any other way the theory that they are lunatics, a right-minded reader is disposed to think that what they have thus seen exists, and that his not having seen such things does not materially diminish that probability.

And here it may be well to recur to the text of these remarks: "Man is not a reasoning animal; he is a seeing, feeling, contemplating, acting animal." All men properly so called—but a good many who walk upright on two legs cannot properly be so called—are seeing, feeling, and acting animals; but very few men, indeed, have as yet attained to be contemplating animals, though the act of contemplation exercised upon the highest objects is, according to all great philosophers, even pagan, the act for which Man is created and in which his final perfection and felicity are attained. The act of real apprehension, as it is exerted by ordinary men, and even for the most part by men of extraordinary vigour of intellectual vision, is momentary, however permanent may be its effect upon their principles and lives. Men of vigorous apprehension look at the heavens of truth, as it were, through a powerful telescope, and see instantly as realities many living lights which are quite invisible to the common eye. But contemplation—a faculty rare in all times, but wellnigh unheard of in ours—is like the photographic plate which finds stars that no telescope can discover, by simply setting its passively expectant gaze in certain indicated directions so long and steadily that telescopically invisible bodies become apparent by accumulation of impression. Such men are prophets and apostles, whether canonical or not. It is by the instrumentality of such men that religions are established and upheld; and the term "verifiable religion" is a piece of mere nineteenth-century cant, when applied to the examination of dogma by such as have probably never had the remotest apprehension of any spiritual reality. Certain facts of history relating to religion may or may not be capable of "verification" to the multitude; but the dogmas which are the substance of a religion can be really apprehended — assuming them to be real and apprehensible—only by the exceedingly few to whom the highest powers of contemplation, which are usually the accompaniments of equally extraordinary virtues, are accorded. The mass of mankind must receive and hold these things as they daily receive and hold a thousand other things—laws, customs, traditions, the grounds of common moralities, etc.—by faith; their real apprehension in such matters extending for the most part only to the discernment of the reasonableness of so receiving and holding them.

Now this faculty and habit of really apprehending things, even in its lower and not uncommon degree, is an immeasurable advantage; but it has its drawback. Those who possess it are singularly capable of committing the unpardonable sin, the sin against knowledge. "Father, forgive them.

for they know not what they do" is a petition which He who spoke these words could not have offered for deeds or denials in clear opposition to what a man knows to be true and good. "My name is in him and He will not pardon." All men agree in calling the spirit of truth—which is the spirit by which truth is really apprehended—holy; and to deny this spirit in deliberate action may, without any appeal to Christian doctrine, be proved to be unpardonable by the way such action is known to influence a man's character. A single act of such denial, if it be in some great and vital matter, often seems to destroy the soul. History affords more than one example of a statesman who has begun life with an eagle eye for truth, a strong and tender love of honour, and everything that makes a man among men. At some crisis of temptation he chooses personal ambition before some clearly apprehended duty of patriotism; and his whole nature seems thenceforward changed: he drops like a scorched fly from the flame—

> Then takes his doom, to limp and crawl,
> Blind and despised, from fall to fall.

But the least practical denial of real apprehension of the truth is, to such as have ever had a conscience and have observed themselves, demonstrably unpardonable, inasmuch as it destroys a portion of the capacity of the soul. "The remnant" may, indeed, "become a great nation," but it will be still and for ever a remnant of what it would have been, had it preserved the integrity of its fidelity.

If we knew the secrets of the lives of those—alas! innumerable—who seem to have no real apprehension of anything, none of the light which, it is said, lighteth every man that cometh into the world, it would probably be found that they have not been born without, but have forfeited, their noblest human heritage by repeated practical denials of the things which they have seen.

XIII

SEERS, THINKERS, AND TALKERS

I

THE intellect, the understanding or discursive reason, and the memory, it need scarcely be said, are three distinct faculties; yet in their exercise and the character they acquire for their possessors, they are apt to be confused, and that not without damage to the public and private interests of those who make the mistake. Intellect, though it is constantly spoken of as synonymous with understanding, is really an incomparably rarer quality, the difference being that which subsists between "genius" and "talent"; and to ignorant persons a ready and well-stored memory, which is consistent with the almost total defect of either of the nobler faculties, is often regarded as a combination of both.

The intellect is the faculty of the "seer." It discerns truth as a living thing; and, according as it is in less or greater power, it discerns with a more or less far-seeing glance the relationships of principles to each other, and of facts, circumstances, and the realities of nature to principles, without anything that can be properly called ratiocination. It cannot be cultivated, as the understanding and memory can be and need to be; and it cannot in the ordinary course of things be injured, except by one means—namely, dishonesty, that is, habitual denial by the will, for the sake of interested or vicious motives, of its own perceptions. Genius and high moral—not necessarily physical—courage are therefore found to be constant companions. Indeed, it is difficult to say how far an absolute moral courage in acknowledging intuitions may not be of the very nature of genius: and whether it might not be described as a sort of interior sanctity which dares to see and confess to itself that it sees, though its vision should place it in a minority of one. Everybody feels that genius is, in a sort, infallible. That it is so, is indeed an "identical proposition." So far as a man is not infallible in what he professes to see, he is not a man of genius—that is, he is not a seer. It is by no figure of speech that genius is called inspiration. Dr. Newman somewhere observes that St. Augustine and some of the primitive teachers of the Church wandered at will through all the mazes of theology with an intuitive orthodoxy of genius.

Although this faculty of direct vision is very rare in comparison with those of ordinary ratiocination and memory, it is not nearly so rare as is supposed by such as measure genius by its manifestations in philosophy, science, art, or statesmanship. For one seer who has the accomplishments and opportunities whereby his faculty can be turned to public account, there are scores and hundreds who possess and exercise for their private use their extraordinary perceptive powers. To whom has it not happened, at one time or other, to witness the instantaneous shattering of some splendid edifice of reasoning and memory by the brief Socratic interrogation of some ignoramus who could see?

No mortal intellect or genius is other than very partial, and, even in that partial character, imperfect. Absolute genius would be nothing more nor less than the sight of all things at once in their relationship and origin; but the most imperfect genius has an infinite value—not only because it is actual sight of truth, but also and still more because it is a peculiar mode of seeing, a reflection of truth coloured but not obscured by the individual character, which in each man of genius is entirely unique. This unique character is, in its expression, what is called "style"—the sure mark of genius, though the world at large is unable to distinguish "style" from manner, or even from mannerism. Incomparably the highest and fortunately the least uncommon form of genius is wisdom in the conduct of life ; for this form involves in a far greater degree than any other the constant exercise of that courage which is inseparable from genius. The saint is simply a person who has so strong and clear a sight of the truth which concerns him individually, and such courage to confess his vision, that he is always ready to become a "confessor" under any extremity of persecution.

True statesmanship is another form of wisdom in the conduct of life; and this is perhaps the rarest of all forms in which genius manifests itself, because it requires a combination of inferior faculties and opportunities which is almost as rare as genius. Poetry is the only near rival of true statesmanship in this respect. The immensely wider and more various range of vision which the great poet exercises when compared with other artists, together with the necessity for the combined working of many lesser faculties and laboriously acquired accomplishments, has always made of the poet the ideal "genius" in the world's esteem. The separate insights into the significance of form, colour, and sound, upon which the arts of the sculptor, painter, and musician are founded, must be included in the vision of the poet of the first rank.

What is called "common sense" is much more nearly allied to genius, or true intellect, either than talent, which is the outcome of the discursive reason, or than learning, which is that of memory. Compared with the sunlight by which the purer intellect sees, common sense is the light of a foggy day, which is good enough to see near objects and to avoid mischief by. Science is generally considered to be the outcome solely of the observation of facts and the discursive reason; but in men like Kepler, Newton, and Faraday there is no lack of "the vision and the faculty divine." The discovery of gravitation by the fall of an apple was pure vision; and it is doubtful whether there was ever a Smith's Prizeman who had not a touch of a higher faculty than that which gropes step by step from premisses to conclusions.

A ghastly semblance of genius is often retained by such persons as once had it, but have ruined it by denying it in action and by endeavouring to prostitute it to selfish or vicious interests. Their judicial blindness is the reverse of that which was inflicted upon Tiresias for daring to gaze upon unveiled wisdom. He could no longer see the world; they can no longer see the heavens. But their original genius takes the perverted form of an intuitive craft in pursuing their ends which is no less amazing, and which, in statesmen especially, is commonly mistaken by the people for the holy faculty which has been quenched.

To be a man of talent a man must be able to think; to be a man of genius he must be able not to think, and especially to abstain from the crazy wool-gathering which is ordinarily regarded as thought. "The harvest of a quiet eye," and the learning of the ear which listens in a silence even of thought, are the wealth of the pure intellect. And the fainter and the more remote the whispers which are heard in such silence, the more precious and potential are they likely to be. It is no condemnation of the thought of Hegel that he is reported to have replied to some question as to the meaning of a passage in his writings, that "he knew what it meant when he wrote it." This thought, too subtle or too simple for expression and memory, might, if held down and compelled to manifest itself more explicitly, have moved mankind.

Genius is a great disturber. It is always a new thing, and demands of old things that they shall make a place for it, which cannot be done without more or less inconvenient rearrangements; and as it seems to threaten even worse trouble than it is finally found to give, it is generally hated and resisted on its first appearance. Moreover, to the eye which is not congenial, the fresh manifestation of genius in almost any kind has something in it alarming and revolting; and it is welcomed with an "Ugh, ugh! the horrid thing! It's alive!" A man of genius who is also a man of sense will never complain of such a reception from his fellows. Their opposition is even respectable from their point of view and with their faculties of beholding.

II

Genius, like sanctity, is commonly more or less foolish in the eyes of the world. Its riches are "the riches of secret places"; and they so much exceed, in its esteem, those that are considered riches by the common sense of men, that its neglect of the ordinary goods of life often amounts to real imprudence—imprudence even from its own point of view, whereby it is bound to avoid hindrances to its free life and exercise. The follies, however, of a Blake or a Hartley Coleridge are venial when compared with those of the thoughtful and prudent fool—the fool in respect of great things, as the other is in respect of small. Who can measure the harm that may be done to the world by a thoughtful and earnest fool—one who starts from data which he is too dull to verify, and who multiplies his mistakes in proportion to the perspicuity and extent of his deductions? The man of "talent" who is merely such, is not a very common phenomenon—for "talent" is in great part the product of culture, which "genius," or the power of seeing, is not. Most persons of talent still possess a share of that obscure kind of genius called common sense, which keeps them from taking up with false principles and following them into wild conclusions. We need, however, only recall some famous figures in the present and past generation in order to be assured that immense talent is consistent with an almost complete deficiency of real insight. When the discursive understanding is in great force and has at its command abundant stores of external information, we behold a power that may work the ruin of empires amid applauding peoples, though it can never build them up. The natural and exact sciences are the proper fields for the exertions of such a faculty.

Stupid persons fancy they derogate from the supremacy of the pure intellect or genius by observing that it is always associated with a vivid imagination, which they regard as a faculty for seeing things as they are not. Shelley made a mistake in a totally different direction when he declared that the imagination is the power by which spiritual things are discerned; whereas the truth is that intellect is the power by which such things are discerned, and imagination is that by which they are expressed. Sensible things alone can be expressed fully and directly by sensible terms. Symbols and parables, and metaphors—which are parables on a small scale—are the only means of adequately conveying, or rather hinting, supersensual knowledge. "He spake not without a parable." Hebrew, Greek, Indian, and Egyptian religions all spoke in parables; and poets deal in images and parables simply because there is no other vehicle for what they have to say. "The things which are unseen may be known by the things which are seen," that is, by way of symbol and parable. Imagination, though it is not, as Shelley says it is, the power of spiritual insight, is its invariable concomitant; and even that dull kinsman of genius, common sense, would feel sadly hampered in its endeavours to convey its perceptions to the minds of others, were it wholly without the faculty of speaking in parables.

It has often been noted that men of genius have bad memories, and that persons having extraordinary memories, like Cardinal Mezzofanti, have little else. The truth is that there are two quite distinct kinds of memory: the memory for external facts and words, apart from their significance; and the memory for spiritual facts and principles. The man of genius, who may have no special reason for cultivating the lower kind of memory, may even find it rather a hindrance than a help. His prayer is, "Let not my heart forget the things mine eyes have seen." So long as his heart retains the significance of the facts he has seen and the words he has heard, he is willing to let the words and the facts go, as a man casts away the shells after he has eaten the oysters. The "well-informed" person commonly differs from the man of genius in this: that he carries about with him all the shells of all the oysters he has ever eaten, and that his soul has grown thin under the burthen.

A commonplace about men of genius is, that they usually have religious dispositions. It would be strange were it otherwise, seeing that genius is nothing but the power of discerning the things of the spirit. The first principle of the most recent form of "psychology" is, indeed, that there is no soul; but that man must have little genius who would not say "Amen" to St. Bernard's epigram, "He must have little spirit who thinks that a spirit is nothing."

After what has just been said, it seems paradoxical to be obliged to admit that the sins to which men of genius are usually most subject are those of sense. From pride, and its offspring envy, hatred, and malice, which play so terrible a part in the affairs of most men, they are comparatively exempt. That they should often be more subject than others to be misled by the ease and pleasure of the senses, may be because the senses of men of genius are more subtly permeated by the spirit, of which they are the ultimate life, than are those of the world at large, and are thereby rendered more acute and less sordidly wicked. This may be said, I hope, without in any way condoning error.

Men of genius, who are therewithal men of cultivated talents and great stores of appropriate information, are the only safe legislators and governors of empires; not only because theirs alone is the sufficiency of sound and far-seeing wisdom, but because they are far less likely than other men to be misled by personal motives and weak fears. But such men, unhappily, are the last to come to the front in states of ultra-popular government; and in such states they have accordingly to suffer that last misery (as by one of the greatest philosophers it has been called), the misery of being governed by worse men than themselves.

XIV

POSSIBILITIES AND PERFORMANCES

IF we take stock of the world's actual achievements—intellectual, moral, and artistic—in the six thousand years during which we know anything about it, it is impossible not to be struck with the extreme smallness of the sum of the acquisitions and attainments of the human race as compared with its desires and apparent possibilities. If those desires and possibilities had in no instances been fulfilled, the entire absence of attainment would have been less startling than is its actual paucity. It would not have been nearly so wonderful if none had reached the high tablelands of excellence in any department of human activity as it is that those heights have been reached by some and by so few. And the marvel of this paucity becomes yet further increased when it is considered that it is not only all that mankind has done, but in all likelihood nearly as much as it could have done had it tried ever so hard. For it is a peculiarity of the very highest work in every kind, that it is not the result of painful labour, but that it is easier to do it than not to do it, when it can be done at all. So that humanity must not be allowed to cover its enormous shortcomings with an " I could an I would." How many philosophers has philosophy produced? If Aristotle be the type, where is the other specimen of the species? How many statesmen have there been whose faculties and characters, nearly inspected, do not provoke the exclamation, " With how little wisdom the world is governed!" In how many Christians has Christianity flowered as in the souls of St. John and St. Francis? Greek architecture and Greek sculpture mean little more than the Parthenon and its friezes. What survives of Greek poetry will scarcely fill one bookshelf, and English poetry, which forms the greater part of the rest of the poetry of the human race, would rest easily on three. The building of the Middle Ages is nothing but the repetition of one inspiration, which would remain transmitted to us almost in its entirety were the Cathedral of Freiburg the only specimen left to us. A single gallery of the Vatican would provide wall-room sufficient for all the paintings of the world that are able to fill with satisfying peace the eye which has been educated by Botticelli, Luini, and Raphael. An ordinary life affords abundant leisure to take in all that two hundred generations of mankind have so done as to fill the craving for what all men feel to be alone satisfyingly human. That is to say, one man in twenty millions or so has been able, during some—often very small—proportion of his life, to be and to do that which all men, when they behold such being and doing, feel to be their natural though utterly unattainable prerogative. Thousands and thousands climb, with praiseworthy struggles and integrity of purpose and with shouts of " Excelsior !", the minor peaks of life ; while two or three in a generation are seen walking with easy breath about those great and tranquil table-lands for which all of us, on beholding them, feel that we were born. It is not that, in a world of inequalities, some two or three in a generation must naturally stand higher than all the rest, as only one among many competitors can be Senior Wrangler. That fuller excellence is a region, and not a pinnacle ; and those who reach it are all upon a great and facile equality, their altitude being simply that of right and unhindered human faculty.

Every individual of the human race is, in this regard, an image of the race itself. Only for a few hours, perhaps, of the million which is about the sum of the longest lifetime, has each one easily and unaccountably found himself to be living indeed. Some accident, some passing occasion which has called upon him to be more than himself, some glimpse of grace in nature or in woman, some lucky disaster even, or some mere wayward tide of existence, has caused the black walls of his prison-house to vanish; and he has breathed in a realm of vision, generosity, and gracious peace, "too transient for delight and too divine." These prophetic moments—one in a million—pass; but, unless he has despised and denied them, they leave him capable, more or less, of understanding prophecy; and he knows that in him also there is a potentiality, realisable perhaps under other than present conditions, of becoming one in that great society in which such states of life appear to be not momentary crises but habits. The wider and the deeper his personal experience of beauty and felicity, the more readily will a man confess that life contains scarcely anything for fruition but abundance for hope; and the better he is acquainted with that which has been best done and said in all ages, the less he will be inclined to believe that the world is making any advances towards the realisation of the promise which every age repeats. An enigma for which science has no key is the certain fact, that if the world be not a prophecy of good things which it shows no likelihood of providing, then it is all nothing but a purposeless and badly conceived tragedy, upon which the sooner the black curtain drops the better. For if the world be not such a prophecy, then the best of men are of all men the most miserable; to these is given beyond others the "transitory gleam" which shows the dulness of their ordinary life for the lingering death it really is; but, knowing little or nothing of life as it is known to such, the stupid and "the wicked have no bonds in their death," and can feel only the comparatively tolerable evils of external and accidental adversity.

There never was a time in which the "higher life," "high art," etc., were less known than in the present, when every goose is gabbling about them. The proof is in the way these names are constantly associated with that of "progress"; whereas progress, as respects the realities, is, if it exists at all, most certainly a progress backwards. The rejoicings of Lord Macaulay and his like over the recent advances of mankind are exactly those of a prosperous shopman over the increase of his business; and the hallelujahs of science are mainly over the elaboration of mighty means for petty ends and of theories which explain away God and exhibit all that past ages have called wisdom as folly. It is too absurd! Yet we must not allow the present eclipse of the electric lights of true learning by the flaring tar-barrels of jubilant ignorance to discourage us in the belief that there is, on the whole, no cessation of the work for which the world goes on. The conscience of mankind, though occasionally confused and obscured, will always cry "Amen" to the great word of St. Augustine, "What ought to be must be"; and the rare achievements of genius and sanctity and the few and far-between glimpses of the life that is indeed life, which are accorded to all, will continue to be accepted as "the substance of things hoped for, the evidence of things not seen."

XV

IMAGINATION

THERE are things which can never be more than approximately defined, and which, even when so defined, are to be rightly understood only in proportion to the degrees in which they are possessed by those who would attempt to comprehend them. Such are, for example, " imagination " and " genius "; which, being faculties that are possessed in a very low degree by nearly all and in a very high degree by extremely few, are matters of the most general interest and the most variable apprehension. That such faculties should, however, as far as possible, be understood is of great practical importance to all persons; inasmuch as it greatly concerns all to know something of the signs, sanctions, and claims of those powers by which they are inevitably more or less ruled externally and internally.

It is nothing against a definition of an entity

IMAGINATION

which cannot be fully defined, to say that such definition is "new." It was objected against an interpretation by St. Augustine of some Old Testament history or parable, that other authorities had given other interpretations. "The more interpretations the better," was the saint's reply. In such cases various definitions and interpretations are merely apprehensions of various sides of a matter not wholly to be embraced or comprehended by any single definition or interpretation. In recent times genius and imagination have come to be widely regarded as one and the same thing. They are not so, however, though they are perhaps indissolubly connected. The most peculiar and characteristic mark of genius is insight into subjects which are dark to ordinary vision and for which ordinary language has no adequate expression. Imagination is rather the language of genius: the power which traverses at a single glance the whole external universe, and seizes on the likenesses and images, and their combinations, which are best able to embody ideas and feelings otherwise inexpressible; so that the "things which are unseen are known by the things which are seen." Imagination, in its higher developments, is so quick and subtle a power that the most delicate analysis can scarcely follow its shortest flights. Coleridge said that it would take a whole volume to analyse the effect of a certain passage of only a few syllables in length. In dealing with such a work as *The Tempest* criticism is absolutely helpless, and its noblest function is to declare its own helplessness by directing attention to beauty beyond beauty which defies analysis. *The Tempest*, like all very great works of art, is the shortest and simplest, and indeed the only possible expression of its "idea." The idea is the product of genius proper; the expression is the work of imagination. There are cases, however, in which it is hard to distinguish at all between these inseparable qualities. The initiation of a scientific theory seems often to have been due to the action of the imagination working independently of any peculiar direct insight; the analogy-discovering faculty—that is, the imagination—finding a law for a whole sphere of unexplained phenomena in the likeness of such phenomena to others of a different sphere of which the law is known. Hence the real discoverers of such theories are scarcely ever those who have obtained the credit of them; for nothing is usually more abhorrent to men of extraordinary imagination than "fact-grinding." Such men, after having flung out their discoveries to the contempt or neglect of their contemporaries, leave the future proof of them to mental mechanics: religiously avoiding such work themselves, lest, as Goethe said of himself, they should find themselves imprisoned in "the charnel-house of science." Genius and imagination of a very high kind are not at all uncommon in children under twelve years of age, especially when their education has been "neglected." The writer can guarantee the following facts from personal witness: A clever child of seven, who could not read, and had certainly never heard of the Newtonian theory of gravitation, said to his mother suddenly, "What makes this ball drop when I leave hold of it?— Oh, I know: the ground pulls it." Another child, a year or two older, lay stretched on a gravel path, staring intently on the pebbles. "They are alive," he cried, in the writer's hearing; "they are always wanting to burst, but something draws them in." This infantine rediscovery of the doctrine of the coinherence of attraction and repulsion in matter seems to have been an effort of direct insight. The repetition of the Newtonian apple revelation seems rather to have been the work of the imagination, tracking likeness in difference; but to discern such likeness is, again, an effort of direct insight, and justifies Aristotle's saying that this power of finding similitude in things diverse is a proof of the highest human faculty. The poet's eye glances from heaven to earth, from earth to heaven; and his faculty of discerning likeness in difference enables him to express the unknown in the terms of the known, so as to confer upon the former a *sensible* credibility, and to give the latter a truly sacramental dignity. The soul contains world upon world of the most real of realities of which it has no consciousness until it is awakened to their existence by some parable or metaphor, some strain of rhythm or music, some combination of form or colour, some scene of beauty or sublimity, which suddenly expresses the inexpressible by a lower likeness. The vulgar cynic, blessing when he only means to bray, declares that love between the sexes is "all imagination." What can be truer? What baser thing is there than such love, when it is not of imagination all compact? or what more nearly divine, when it is? Why? Because the imagination deals with the spiritual realities to which the material realities correspond, and of which they are only, as it were, the ultimate and sensible expressions. And here it may be noted, by the way, that Nature supplies the ultimate analogue of every divine mystery with some vulgar use or circumstance, in order, as it would seem, to enable the stupid and the gross to deny the divine without actual blasphemy.

Profligacy and "fact-grinding" destroy the

imagination by habitually dwelling in ultimate expressions while denying or forgetting the primary realities of which they are properly only the vessels. Purity ends by finding a goddess where impurity concludes by confessing carrion. Which of these is the reality let each man judge according to his taste. "Fact-grinding"—which Darwin confessed and lamented had destroyed his imagination and caused him to "nauseate Shakespeare"—commonly ends in destroying the religious faculty, as profligacy destroys the faculty of love ; for neither love nor religion can survive without imagination, which Shelley, in one of his prefaces, identifying genius with imagination, declares to be the power of discerning spiritual facts. Those who have no imagination regard it as all one with "fancy," which is only a playful mockery of imagination, bringing together things in which there is nothing but an accidental similarity in externals.

XVI

THE LIMITATIONS OF GENIUS

IN art, as in higher matters, "strait is the gate, and narrow is the way which leadeth unto life, and few there be that find it;" and the initial cause of failure in many who seem to have faculties which should ensure success, is not so much the difficulty of the road which leads to it as want of humility in confessing its narrowness. Each man is by birth a unique individuality, which the circumstances of his life will increase and develop continually, if he be content to do his duty in the station, intellectual and otherwise, to which it has pleased God to call him, without falling below its obligations or assuming others which have not been laid upon him. The low but still priceless degree of genius which consists in individuality in manners, and which renders the possessor of it powerfully though imperceptibly edifying in all companies, is open to all, though few are sufficiently simple and honest and unambitious to attain to it by turning neither to the right hand nor the left in pursuit of their particular good of life.

"Originality," whether in manners, action, or art, consists simply in a man's being upon his own line; in his advancing with a single mind towards his unique apprehension of good; and in his doing so in harmony with the universal laws which secure to all men the liberty of doing as he is doing, without hindrance from his or any other's individuality. Unless "originality" thus works in submission to and harmony with general law, it loses its nature. In morals it becomes sin or insanity, in manners and in art oddity and eccentricity, which are in reality the extreme opposites and travesties of originality. As in religion it is said that "no man can know whether he is worthy of love," so in art and ordinary life no man can know whether he is original. If through habitual fidelity to his idea of good he has attained to originality, he will be the last person in the world to know it. If he thinks he is original, he is probably not so; and if he is commonly praised for originality, he may hardly hope to attain to any such distinction. Originality never expresses itself in harsh and obtrusive singularities. A society of persons of true originality in manners would be like an oak-tree, the leaves of which all look alike until they are carefully compared, when it is found that they are all different. In art, the sphere of extraordinary originalities, there is the same absence of strongly pronounced distinctions, and therefore the same withdrawal from the recognition of the vulgar, who look for originality in antics, oddities, crudities, and incessant violations of the universal laws which true originality religiously observes; its very function consisting, as it does, in upholding those laws and illustrating them and making them unprecedentedly attractive by its own peculiar emphases and modulations.

The individuality or "genius" of a man, which results from fidelity in life and art to his "ruling love," is almost necessarily narrow. Shakespeare is the only artist that ever lived whose genius has even approached to universality. His range is so great that ordinary readers, if, like Mr. Frederic Harrison, they had the courage to speak their impressions, would with him condemn the greater part of the poet's work as "rubbish"—that is, as having no counterpart in the "positivism" of their actual or imaginative experience. Every play of Shakespeare is a new vision—not only a new aspect of his vision, as is the case with the different works of nearly all other artists, even the greatest.

Narrowness, indeed, so far from being opposed

to greatness in art, is often its condition. Dante and Wordsworth are proofs that greatness of genius consists in seeing clearly rather than much; and well it would have been both for poets and for readers had the former always or even generally understood the economy of moving always on their own lines. Nothing has so much injured modern art as the artist's ambition to show off his "breadth"; and many an immortal lyric or idyll has been lost because the lyric or idyllic poet has chosen to forsake his line for the production of exceedingly mortal epics or tragedies. The modern custom of exhibiting all the works of a single painter at a time affords proof which every one will understand of what has been said. Who, with an eye for each painter's true quality, can have gone over the collections in recent years of the pictures of Reynolds, Rossetti, Blake, Holman Hunt, and others, without a feeling of surprise, and some perhaps irrational disappointment, at the discovery for the first time of the artist's limitations? Each had painted the same vision over and over again! There was no harm in that. The mistake was in bringing together the replicas which should have adorned "palace chambers far apart." But poets, whose "works" are always collectively exhibited, should beware how they betray the inevitable fact of the narrowness of genius. Not only should they never leave their own line for another which is not their own, but they should be equally careful not to go over it again when they have once got to the end of it.

XVII

A "PESSIMIST" OUTLOOK

DESPOTISM, which is not government, but anarchy speaking with one voice, whether it be the mandate of an irresponsible emperor or that of a multitude, is the "natural" death of all nationalities. They may die by other means, but this is the end they come to if left to themselves. When this end is reached, the corrupt body may, for a time, preserve a semblance of its old identity; but it is no longer a nation: it is merely a localisation of "man's shameful swarm," in which the individual has no help from the infinitely greater and nobler vitality of which he was a living member to erect himself above himself, and to breathe the generous breath, and feel himself in all his acts a partaker of the deceased giant's superhuman vigour. The incidence of the misery is not only upon those comparatively few who may be conscious of its cause. The malaria of the universal marsh stupefies the brain and deadens the heart of the very ploughman who turns its sod, and he is hourly the worse for want of the healthy breeze and invigorating prospect of the ancient hills, which he himself was, perhaps, among the most eager to level. Though he knew it not, he was every day sensibly the better for being the member of a great nation.

> "He felt the giant's heat,
> Albeit he simply called it his,
> Flush in his common labour with delight,
> And not a village maiden's kiss
> But was for this
> More sweet,
> And not a sorrow but did lightlier sigh,
> And for its private self less greet,
> The while that other so majestic self stood by."

If he does not feel the loss of his corporate life, but is content to struggle, stink, and sting with the rest of the swarm into which the national body has been resolved by corruption, so much the worse for him. His insensibility is the perfection of his misery. To others, not so lost, there may be hope, though not in this stage of being. None who has ever lived through the final change, or who, being in the foul morass of resulting "equality," has been able to discern what national life means, can find in private fortune—wife, children, friends, money—any compensation for the great life of which his veins are empty. He knows that there is no proximate hope, no possibility of improvement in such a state of things. He knows that it is absurd to expect anything from "education" of the mass. True education cannot exist under either kind of despotism. National life is the beginning and end of individual culture, as far as this world is concerned. The acquisition of knowledge by an unorganised or enslaved multitude, which must always be, in the main, self-seeking and unjust, is merely the acquisition of subtler and baser means for the advancement of individual covetousness and the indulgence of individual vices. Such education is but "a jewel in a swine's snout." Fools may fill the air with sentimental or hypocritical "aspirations" for the good of the community; but no community exists where no excellence has the power of asserting itself politically and more or less in spite of the ignorance and malice of those whom it would serve. Such "aspirations" are but the iridescent colours on the stagnant pool; putrid splendours which have no existence in the chronic and salutary storm of national life.

Nor is there any hope from without. A comparatively savage people has often been impregnated with the germ of national being by the military invasion of a civilisation still in the vigour of growth; but there is no instance of a civilisation which has thus lapsed into anarchy having been regenerated by any such means, though its stagnated life may have been perpetuated, as in the case of China, by an external tyranny more powerful than any of the shifting forms of despotism which it develops, if left to itself, from within. Nor is there any light, even in the far future, unless for him who has a fulness of that cosmopolitan benevolence which is so often the boast of the simpleton or the political hypocrite, but, happily, so seldom the possession of the natural man. He knows that no soil has ever yet been found to bear two crops of national life, though the corruption of one has often been found, after many generations of consummated decay, to be very useful dung for the nourishment of other and far removed fields. But this consideration does not bring him within measurable distance of practical political consolation.

The frantic ambition of one bad man, and the cowardice of half a dozen others, who would have been honest had it not appeared too personally inconvenient, and the apathy of that large portion of the community which has been sane in judgment but insane in sloth, have brought the final evil upon us fifty or a hundred years sooner than it need have come. But come it must have done sooner or later, since the powers of evil have invariably, in worldly matters, proved too strong in the long run for those of good; and such as cannot bear this truth, but require that abiding temporal good should come of their good works, had better go into monasteries. Considering what men are, the wonder is, not that all great nationalities should have come to a shameful end, but that their ordinary duration of life should have been a thousand years. How any of them should have lasted a hundred must seem a miracle to those who fail to take into account the agency of the two guardian angels of national life, religion and war—religion which keeps alive the humility and generosity of reasonable submission to law and the spirit of self-sacrifice for corporate life; and war, which silences for a time the envy and hatred of the evil and ignorant for moral and circumstantial superiorities, and compels them to trust their established leaders on pain of prompt annihilation.

Even our great "liberal" prophet, Mr. Herbert Spencer, is compelled, in spite of himself, to prophesy with terror of what he rightly calls "the coming slavery," the despotism, not of a single irresponsible tyrant, who must content himself with doing good or evil in so general a way that the sense of private compulsion or injury would weigh little on each individual, but the paltry and prying despotism of the vestry—the more "virtuous" the more paltry and prying—persecuting each individual by the intrusion of its myriad-handed, shifting, ignorant, and irresistible tyranny into the regulation of our labour, our household, and our very victuals, and, however "pure" in its abstract intention, necessarily corrupt in its application by its agents, since men, as a rule, are corrupt. Indications are not wanting of the sort of "government" we are committed to, unless the coming war shall leave us in the grip of a less irksome tyranny. It will be a despotism which will have to be mitigated by continual "tips," as the other kind has had to be by occasional assassination. Neither the voter nor the inspector yet know their power and opportunities; but they soon will. We shall have to "square" the district surveyor once or twice a year, lest imaginary drains become a greater terror than real typhoid; we shall have to smoke our pipes secretly and with a sense of sin, lest the moral supervisor of the parish should decline our offer of half-a-crown for holding his nose during his weekly examination of our bedrooms and closets; the good Churchman will have to receive Communion under the "species" of ginger-ale— as some advanced congregations have already proposed—unless the parson can elude the church-warden with white port, or otherwise persuade him; and, every now and then, all this will be changed, and we shall have to tip our policemen and inspectors for looking over our infractions of popular moralities of a newer pattern. Our condition will very much resemble Swedenborg's hell, in which everybody is incessantly engaged in the endeavour to make everybody else virtuous; and the only compensating comforts to the sane will be that, though wine and tobacco, those natural stimulants to good impulses and fruitful meditations, may be denied him, he may find abundant time and opportunity, in the cessation of all external interests of a moral and intellectual nature, for improving his own character, which, perhaps, is, after all, the only way in which a man can be sure of improving the world's; and, furthermore, he will no longer be discomposed by the prospect of "national disaster," since there can be no national disaster where there is no nation, however freely the gutters may run with blood. Private disaster, in such an infernal millennium, will be a trifle.

Under such conditions, secret societies of discontented and hopeless minorities will abound. Dynamite will often shake the nerves of smug content, and enrage the People beyond bounds at such revolt against its infallible decrees. But none of these societies will be so hateful as the secret and inevitable aristocracy of the remnant that refuses to give interior assent to the divinity of the Brummagem Baal. Its members will acquire means of association and methods of forbidding intrusion which will infuriate the rest, who, in their turn, will invent tests for the discovery, in order to the punishment, of these "enemies of mankind," as the Dutch traders in Japan did, in inviting all persons of doubtful character to trample on the crucifix.

I have called these glances at the near future "pessimist," because that is the word now generally applied to all such forecasts as are made by those who do not ignore or pervert patent facts. "Optimists," as far as I can gather, are those who hope all things from "local option."

XVIII

THOUGHTS ON KNOWLEDGE, OPINION, AND INEQUALITY

SOME learned men have maintained that we can know nothing. The truth is better stated by St. Paul: "If a man thinks that he knows anything, he knows nothing as he ought," that is nothing other than imperfectly. It is the more difficult to deal systematically with this matter, because we want, in our tongue, words of such relative meaning as *scire, cognoscere, intelligere,* etc. I propose only to run together a few such observations as simple good sense can make, and accept, and find use for.

A great and increasing proportion of persons would, if you asked them, maintain that all convictions are merely opinions. But it is not so. A fool may opine absolutely that a wise man is a fool, but the wise man knows that the fool is one. The same or opposite conclusions, political or otherwise, may be arrived at by two persons from a view of the same facts, and each may be equally confident; but the conclusions of one may be knowledge, and those of the other opinion. The reality of the difference is indicated by the difference of the feelings which commonly subsist between those who opine and those who know. Those who opine hate those who know, and who speak as those who know. They think it an assumption of superiority, whereas it is only its reality, and cannot but appear more or less in its manner of expression. Those who know, are contemptuous or indifferent only towards such as impudently or ignorantly opine. The consequence is that the knowledge which is wisdom is nowhere as an acknowledged force and factor in worldly affairs, and is able to assert itself only *sub rosa*, or by accident, or by the more or less underhand management of folly and ignorance.

What most people call " deep and earnest convictions" on political and social topics are generally muddle-headed medleys of knowledge of fact and opinion. They know that such and such a thing is an evil, and they opine that they see a way to amend it; and if wiser people point out to them that the evil would not be so amended, or that greater evils would accrue from the attempt, they only feel that their " convictions " are affronted and opposed by cold-blooded calculations. This kind of opinion is often as confident as actual knowledge. When Carlyle said that it was impossible to believe a lie, he can only have meant that it was impossible to believe it with that highest kind of certitude which consists in intellectual perception. Probably no one could believe a lie with that degree of faith which would enable him to suffer deliberate martyrdom for it. Protestant and Catholic martyrs have usually been sufferers for one and the same faith, or, at least, parts of the same faith, in which parts they have considered the whole to be involved. Very few, if any, have ever carried the courage of mere "opinions" to the stake.

There can be no absolute certitude about the impressions of the senses or the inferences drawn from them. There can be about moral and spiritual things. The knave may sincerely opine that it is best for his interests to lie and cheat; but the honest man knows that he is a being whose interests are above all external contingencies, and that under certain circumstances it would be madness to behave otherwise than in a way which would be directly opposed to every argument and persuasion of the senses. It is only the mind of the most highly "scientific" constitution that will have its confidence in knowledge of this kind tried by considerations of its moral and intellectual obligations to Hottentots and Australian aborigines. "We can live in houses without being architects"; and we can know, without knowing or caring to know how we came by our knowledge. The house of the gods has lasted intact since Abraham and Hesiod, and shows no sign yet of tumbling about our ears.

The faculty of knowing, as differing from that of opining, seems, as might be expected from what has been said, to have as much to do with the character of the will as with that of the mind. To be honest, Shakespeare tells us, is to be one in ten thousand; and to discern intellectually, or to know, is a part, and a very great part, of honesty. A man may have learned a dozen languages, and have the whole circle of the sciences at his fingers' ends, and may know nothing worthy of being called knowledge; indeed, there is nothing which seems to be a greater hindrance to the acquisition of living knowledge than an engrossing devotion to the acquisition of words, facts, logical methods, and natural laws. It requires little learning to make a wise or truly knowing man, but much learning may not impossibly spoil one.

Mr. Matthew Arnold has said that a thorough classical education has often the same effects on a man's character as a grave experience. The reason is that it is a grave experience, a long series of small exercises of honesty, patience, and self-sacrifice, the sum of which is equal to a great and soul-sobering calamity. The author of the *Imitation* notes a kindred fact when he says, "No man can know anything till he is tried." Not only is the discipline of such an education, which, in its early stage at least, has much in it that is repugnant and compulsory, fitted to qualify the character for the reception of true knowledge, but it conveys also, in an eminent degree, the matter of true knowledge. Without any disrespect to Professor Huxley, Mr. Herbert Spencer, and Professor Max Müller, we may affirm that the man who knew Plato, Homer, and Æschylus rightly, and knew little else, would know far more than he who knew all that these great scientists could teach, and knew nothing else.

The man who knows, often finds himself at great disadvantage in the presence of fact-gatherers and persons who opine. His attitude is necessarily affirmative, and often, to the great scandal and contempt of his adversaries, simply affirmative. It does not enter into his calculations to have to defend actively a position which he sees to be impregnable; and when he leaves his proper occupation of "climbing trees in the Hesperides" to wield his club against those who know of no such trees, he is like a Hercules fighting mosquitoes. They cannot even see his club, and the conflict generally ends, as did that between the Lady and Comus with an angry and wholly unconvincing assertion of incompetence.

> Fain would I something say, yet to what end?
> Thou hast nor ear, nor soul to apprehend
> The sublime notion and high mystery
> That must be utter'd to unfold the sage
> And serious doctrine of virginity.
> And thou art worthy that thou should'st not know
> More happiness than is thy present lot.
> Enjoy your dear wit and gay rhetoric,
> That hath so well been taught her dazzling fence;
> Thou art not fit to hear thyself convinced.

Wordsworth, in a still greater passion, calls his scientific adversary "a fingering slave." Of course this sort of thing tends to make the relations of the parties unpleasant; and in the eyes of the world the man of immense "information" and convinced ignorance goes off with the laurels.

Metaphysics for the most part are justly open to the objection that they attempt to explain things which Aristotle declares to be too simple to be intelligible—things which we cannot see with definiteness, not because they are beyond the focus of the mind's eye, but because they are too much within it. The metaphysician Hegel says that the sense of honour arises from our consciousness of infinite personal value. This may not be wholly satisfactory, but it is helpful; it is a part of the truth. But what do physicists make of such things as honour and chastity? They certainly endeavour to explain such ideas and feelings as they do everything else, but their explanations necessarily discredit these and all other things which profess to have "infinite value," and which wise men know to have infinite value.

The knowledge which can be made common to all, is a foundation upon which a certain increasing school, finding popular "opinion" too sandy, is endeavouring to build up a new state of things, religious, moral, political, and social. This kind of "positivism," which claims for its sanction the common, that is to say, the lowest experience of mankind, is and always has been the religion of the vulgar, to whatever class they belong. The growth of an unconscious and undogmatic positivism among the people at large is perhaps the most notable fact of the time. It shows itself not only in an increasing impatience of the notion that there is any reality which cannot be seen and felt, but in an intolerance even of any experience which is not, or cannot immediately be made, the experience of all. As boards and committees proverbially have to work on the level of the least wise of their members, so the ideal perfection of this positivism would be government by the insight of the greatest dunderhead, since his experiences and perceptions alone would be sufficiently communicable to have the character of universality. Under such ideal conditions, every reality that makes life human would be completely eliminated. A man who should be detected in secretly entertaining principles of abstract honour, or trying to form his life upon the pattern of a beauty unknown to the arch-dunderhead, would fare as it fared in Athens with the man who dared to crown his house with a pediment; and vestries, consisting of the prophets of commonplace and popular experience, would vote everything in painting and poetry to be "bosh" which should be more esoteric in character than Frith's "Railway Station" or Martin Tupper's *Proverbial Philosophy*.

Science has already come very generally to mean, not that which may be known, but only such knowledge as every animal with faculties a little above those of an ant or a beaver can be induced to admit. Incommunicable knowledge, or knowledge which can be communicated at present only to a portion—perhaps a small portion—of mankind, is already affirmed to be no knowledge at all. A man who knows and acts up to his knowledge that it is better to suffer or inflict any extremity of temporal evil, than to lie or cheat, though he may not be able to give any universally intelligible account of his knowledge, is already beginning to be looked upon as a prig or a fanatic; and chastity is already widely declared to be one of the "dead virtues," and marriage only legalised fornication, because "the sublime notion and high mystery that must be uttered to unfold the sage and serious doctrine" of purity must be taken, if taken at all by the many, upon trust.

The pure and simple ideal of life founded upon facts of universal experience is, however, too base ever to be perfectly attained in this world. There will always be a lingering suspicion with many that some have powers of discernment and an experience which are not granted to all; there will always be hidden heretics who will believe that there are realities which cannot be seen or touched by the natural eye or hand, or even by the rational perception of the many; and the present downward tendency may perhaps be checked, or at least delayed, by recalling to the minds of men that, as yet, we are all living more or less by faith in the better knowledge of the few, and by reminding them of that abyss towards which a new step is taken whenever any item of that knowledge is denied in order to widen the foundations of the throne of popular experience.

The religion of universal experience must of course begin, as the dogmatic positivist insists, in the denial of God, or, what is exactly equivalent, in the assertion that, if God exists, He is altogether unknowable and removed from the practical interests of life. Now, let it be remembered that for a man to deny that God can be known is quite a different thing from his not being able to affirm, from positive knowledge, the reverse. A very small minority of mankind, but a minority which includes almost all who have attained the highest peaks of heroic virtue and many who have been no less eminent for power of intellect and practical wisdom, have declared that, to them at least, God is knowable, communicable with, and personally discernible with a certainty which exceeds all other certainties; and they have further affirmed that this knowledge comes and can only come from a man's putting himself *en rapport* with the Divinity by an, in the beginning, more or less experimental faith, and by a conformity to the dictates of the highest conscience, so perfect as to involve, for a considerable period at least, laborious and painful self-denial. Now it would be placing oneself upon a level with such assertors of the highest knowledge to say that one knows that these declarations are true, however strong the presumption of their truth may appear; but it is simply vulgar and brutal impudence for any one to assert positively that they are untruths or illusions, merely because his own experience or that of his pot-companions contains nothing which gives the least clue to their meaning. The *reductio ad absurdum* becomes complete when the same argument is carried into regions of more extended experience. A drunken bargeman has exactly the same right to deny the reality of the asserted experiences of a Petrarch or a Wordsworth as these would have to deny those of the saint or the apostle; and to descend a few steps farther, the amateur of abominable delights and the violator of natural relationships would justly, upon the widest experimental grounds, claim exemption from a condemnation chiefly founded upon an obscure perception and an intuitive horror of which he for his part had no experience.

Popular positivism will, however, always stop short of the length to which the doctrines of its prophets would lead it, and will, from time to time, be beaten back into the paths of the positivism of the nobler few on which all virtue and religion are founded, by finding itself in contact with the tremendous paradox, that the most universally beneficial and admired fruits of civilisation are and always have been gathered from trees of which the roots are wholly out of common view. The heroes themselves of the people will always refute popular experience better than any philosopher can. Though a Gladstone may dazzle them for a day by investing with a fatuous glamour the principles and platitudes with which the vulgar are familiar, it is to a Gordon, with inimitable courage and honour, the obvious outcome of unintelligible thoughts and experiences, that they will look with abiding reverence and an elevating instinct that such men habitually move about in worlds by them unrealised.

The immense and unalterable inequalities in the knowing faculties of man are the source and in part the justification of that social inequality which roughly and very partially reflects them. Many otherwise amiable and conservative thinkers have, however, made the mistake of conceding that such inequality is, abstractedly considered, an evil, though a hopelessly incurable one. Conservative teaching would be much more effective than it is were it more frequently occupied with proving that such inequality is no evil, but a very great good for all parties.

Dr. Johnson, who sometimes let fall, in off-hand talk, sayings of such depth, simplicity, and significance that we must go back to the philosophers of antiquity to find the like of them, once remarked that " inequality is the source of all delight." This saying, which must seem surprising to most modern ears, is absolutely true and even demonstrable.

All delight—not all pleasure, which is quite a different thing—will be found, when thoroughly examined, to consist in the rendering and receiving of love and the services of love. Hence the great and fortunately inextinguishable fountains of delight in the relationships of man and woman and of parents and children. It is true that a low and inorganic form of national polity may, to some extent, suppress even these pure springs of felicity; but, so long as there are women and children in the world, it can never become quite joyless. The doctrines of liberty, fraternity, and equality are known instinctively only by very bad children; and most women, when once they have been in love, repudiate such teaching indignantly, under whatever polity they may have been born.

>   Between unequals sweet is equal love;

and the fact is that there is no love, and therefore no sweetness, which is not thus conditioned; and the greater the inequality the greater the sweetness. Hence the doctrine that infinite felicity can arise only from the mutual love of beings infinitely unequal—that is, of the creator and the creature. Inequality, far from implying any dishonour on either side of the mutual compact of love, is the source of honour to both. Hooker, writing of marriage, says: "It is no small honour to a man that a creature so like himself should be subjected to him"; and we all know that the honour to woman which the chivalry of the middle ages made an abiding constituent of civilisation, was founded upon Catholic views of her subjection, and the obligation to give special honour, as of right, to the weaker vessel. Look also at the relations which usually subsist between an hereditary gentleman and his hereditary unequals and dependants, and compare them with the ordinary fraternal relations between a Radical master-tradesman and his workmen. The intercourse between the gentleman and his hind or labourer is free, cheerful, and exhilarating, because there is commonly in it the only equality worth regarding, that of goodwill; whereas the commands of the sugar-boiler or the screw-maker to their brothers are probably given with a frown and received with a scowl. Social inequality, since it arises from unalterable nature and inevitable chance, is irritating only when it is not recognised. The American plutocrat may be forced to travel for a week in the company of a hodman, because

American theories discountenance first and third class carriages; but catch him speaking to him! Whereas an English duke, if by chance thrown into the companionship of an honest countryman, would be on the best of terms with him before an hour was over, and the good understanding between the two would be made all the easier should the latter have on his distinguishing smock-frock. The genuine Tory is the most accessible of persons, the genuine Radical the least so. The one takes things as they are and must be, the other views them as they are not and cannot be, and, kicking against imaginary evils, often pays the penalty of finding himself firmly saddled with the realities.

"One can live in a house without being an architect," and it is not at all necessary that the common people should understand the English constitution in order to feel that their lives are the sweeter and nobler because they are members of its living organism. Not a ploughboy or a milkmaid but would feel, without in the least knowing why, that a light had passed from their lives with the disappearance of social inequalities, and the consequent loss of their dignity as integral parts of a somewhat that was greater than themselves.

The other day, walking in a country lane, I saw what appeared at a little distance to be a dying animal. On a closer view it proved to be the carcase of a sheep which had in great measure been actually transformed into a mass of the soft, white, malodorous grubs known to anglers by the name of gentles. The struggles of these creatures to get at the food which they concealed produced a strong and regular pulsation throughout the whole mass, and gave it a ghastly semblance of breathing. The ordered state of England, according to its ideal, which for many generations has been more or less realised, compared with the sort of democracy to which we are fast drifting and have wellnigh attained, is much like the animal in which myriads of individual organs, nerves, veins, tissues, and cells formed subordinated parts of one living thing, compared with this pulsating mass of grubs, each one of which had no thought but of its just share of carrion.

Democracy is only a continually shifting aristocracy of money, impudence, animal energy, and cunning, in which the best grub gets the best of the carrion; and the level to which it tends to bring all things is not a mountain tableland, as its promoters would have their victims think, but the unwholesome platitude of the fen and the morass, of which black envy would enjoy the malaria so long as all others shared in it. Whatever may be the pretences set forth by the leading advocates of such a state of things among us, it is manifest enough that black envy is the principal motive with many of them, who hate the beauty of the ordered life to be ruling stars of which they cannot attain, just as certain others are said to "hate the happy light from which they fell." They hate hereditary honours, chiefly because they produce hereditary honour and create a standard of truth and courage for which even the basest are the better in so far as they are shamed by it. Do the United States, some may ask, justify this condemnation? They are but a poor approach to the idea of democracy which seems now about to be realised among us: but they have already gone a long way towards extinguishing that last glory of, and now best substitute for, a generally extinct religion—a sense of honour among the people. "Why, what a dern'd fool you must be!" exclaimed a New York shopkeeper to a friend of mine, who had received a dollar too much in changing a note, and returned it. If there is a shopkeeper in England who would think such a thing, there is certainly not one who would dare to say it.

Nor, in losing sight of the sense of "infinite personal value," which is the source of honour and the growth of a long-enduring recognition of inevitable inequalities, have the Americans preserved delight. Dr. Johnson's saying finds a remarkable comment in the observation of a recent American traveller: "In the United States there is everywhere comfort, but no joy."

To conclude, it is quite possible to change the forms of social inequality, but to do away with the fact is of all things the most impossible. It is the trick or ignorance of the demagogue to charge existing inequalities with the evils and injustices in which they began, and with which they were attended for a long time afterwards. When conquest or revolution establishes the ever-inevitable political and social inequalities in new forms, it takes many generations of misery and turmoil to introduce into them the moral equality which renders them not only tolerable, but the source of true freedom and happiness.

XIX

LOVE AND POETRY

EVERY man and woman who has not denied or falsified nature knows, or at any rate feels, that love, though the least "serious," is the most significant of all things. The wise do not talk much about this knowlege, for fear of exposing its delicate edge to the stolid resistance of the profligate and unbelieving, and because its light, though, and for the reason that, it exceeds all other, is deficient in definition. But they see that to this momentary transfiguration of life all that is best in them looks forward or looks back, and that it is for this the race exists, and not this for the race—the seed for the flower, not the flower for the seed. All religions have sanctified this love, and have found in it their one word for and image of their fondest and highest hopes; and the Catholic has exalted it into a "great Sacrament," holding that, with Transubstantiation—which it resembles—it is unreasonable only because it is above reason. "The love which is the best ground of marriage," writes also the Protestant and "judicious" Hooker, "is that which is least able to render a reason for itself." Indeed, the extreme unreasonableness of this passion, which gives cause for so much blaspheming to the foolish, is one of its surest sanctions and a main cause of its inexhaustible interest and power; for who but a "scientist" values greatly or is greatly moved by anything he can understand—that which can be comprehended being necessarily less than we are ourselves?

In this matter the true poet must always be a mystic—altogether to the vulgar, and more or less to all who have not attained to his peculiar knowledge. For what is a mystery but that which one does not know? The common handicrafts used to be called mysteries; and their professors were mystics to outsiders exactly in the sense that poets or theologians, with sure, but to them uncommunicated and perhaps incommunicable, knowledge, are mystics to the many. The poet simply knows more than they do; but it flatters their malignant vanity to call him names which they mean to be opprobrious, though they are not, because he is not such a spiritual pauper as themselves. But poets are mystics, not only by virtue of knowledge which the greater part of mankind does not possess, but also because they deal with knowledge against which the accusation of dunces who know the differential calculus is etymologically true—namely, that it is *absurd*. Love is eternally absurd, for that which is the root of all things must itself be without root. Aristotle says that things are unintelligible to man in proportion as they are simple; and another says, in speaking of the mysteries of love, that the angels themselves desire in vain to look into these things.

In the hands of the poet, mystery does not hide knowledge, but reveals it as by its proper medium. Parables and symbols are the only possible modes of expressing realities which are clear to perception though dark to the understanding. "Without a parable he spake not" who always spake of primary realities. Every spiritual reality fades into something else, and none can tell the point at which it fades. The only perfectly definite things in the universe are the conceptions of a fool, who would deny the sun he lives by if he could not see its disc. Natural sciences are definite, because they deal with laws which are not realities but conditions of realities. The greatest and perhaps the only real use of natural science is to supply similes and parables for poets and theologians.

But if the realities of love were not in themselves dark to the understanding, it would be necessary to darken them—not only lest they should be profaned, but also because, as St. Bernard says, "The more the realities of heaven are clothed with obscurity, the more they delight and attract, and nothing so much heightens longing as such tender refusal." "Night," says the inspirer of St. Bernard, "is the light of my pleasures."

Love is rooted deeper in the earth than any other passion; and for that cause its head, like that of the Tree Igdrasil, soars higher into heaven. The heights demand and justify the depths, as giving them substance and credibility. "That He hath ascended—what is it but because He first also descended into the lower parts of the earth?" Love "reconciles the highest with the lowest, ordering all things strongly and sweetly from end to end." St. Bernard says that "divine love" (religion) "has its first root in the most secret of the human affections." This affection is the only key to the inner sanctuaries of that faith which declares, "Thy Maker is thy Husband;" the only clue by which searchers of the "secret of the King," in the otherwise inscrutable writings of prophet and apostle, discover, as Keble writes, "the loving hint that meets the longing guess," which looks to the future for the satisfying and abiding reality, the passage of whose momentary shadow forms the supreme glory of our mortality.

The whole of after-life depends very much upon how life's transient transfiguration in youth by love is subsequently regarded; and the greatest of all the functions of the poet is to aid in his readers the fulfilment of the cry, which is that of nature as well as religion, "Let not my heart forget the things mine eyes have seen." The greatest perversion of the poet's function is to falsify the memory of that transfiguration of the senses and to make light of its sacramental character. This character is instantly recognised by the unvitiated heart and apprehension of every youth and maiden; but it is very easily forgotten and profaned by most, unless its sanctity is upheld by priests and poets. Poets are naturally its prophets—all the more powerful because, like the prophets of old, they are wholly independent of the priests, and are often the first to discover and rebuke the lifelessness into which that order is always tending to fall. If society is to survive its apparently impending dangers, it must be mainly by guarding and increasing the purity of the sources in which society begins. The world is finding out, as it has often done before, and more or less forgotten, that it cannot do without religion.

Love is the first thing to wither under its loss. What love does in transfiguring life, that religion does in transfiguring love: as any one may see who compares one state or time with another. Love is sure to be something less than human if it is not something more; and the so-called extravagances of the youthful heart, which always claims a character for divinity in its emotions, fall necessarily into sordid, if not shameful, reaction, if those claims are not justified to the understanding by the faith which declares man and woman to be priest and priestess to each other of relations inherent in Divinity itself, and proclaimed in the words "Let us make man in our own image" and "male and female created he them." Nothing can reconcile the intimacies of love to the higher feelings unless the parties to them are conscious—and true lovers always are—that, for the season at least, they justify the words "I have said, Ye are gods." Nuptial love bears the clearest marks of being nothing other than the rehearsal of a communion of a higher nature. "Its felicity consists in a perpetual conversion of phase from desire to sacrifice, and from sacrifice to desire, accompanied by unchangeable complaisance in the delight shining in the beauty of the beloved; and it is agitated in all its changes by fear, without which love cannot long exist as emotion."

Such a state, in proportion to its fervour, delicacy, and perfection, is ridiculous unless it is regarded as a "great sacrament." It is the inculcation of this significance which has made love between man and woman what it is now—at least to the idea and aspirations of all good minds. It is time that the sweet doctrine should be enforced more clearly. Love being much more respected and religion much less than of old, the danger of profanation is not so great as it was when religion was revered and love despised. The most characteristic virtue of woman, or at least the most alluring of her weaknesses—her not caring for masculine truth and worth unless they woo her with a smile or a touch or some such flattery of her senses—is the prevailing vice of most men, especially in these times. This general effeminacy is the poet's great opportunity. It is his pontifical privilege to *feel* the truth; and his function is to bridge the gulf between severe verity and its natural enemy, feminine sentiment, by speech which, without any sacrifice of the former, is "simple, sensuous, and passionate." He insinuates in nerve-convincing music the truths which the mass of mankind must feel before they believe. He leads them by their affections to things above their affections, making Urania acceptable to them by her prænomen Venus. He is the apostle of the Gentiles, and conveys to them, without any flavour of cant or exclusiveness, the graces which the chosen people have too often denied or disgraced in their eyes.

XX

THE WEAKER VESSEL

IT is "of faith" that the woman's claim to the honour of man lies in the fact of her being the "weaker vessel." It would be of no use to prove what every Christian man and woman is bound to believe, and what is, indeed, obvious to the senses of any sane man and woman whatever. But a few words of random comment on the text may, by adding to faith knowledge, make man and woman—woman especially—more thankful than before for those conditions which constitute the chief felicity of her life and his, and which it is one of the chief triumphs of progress to render ever more and more manifest. The happiest result of the "higher education" of woman cannot fail to consist in the rendering of her weakness more and more daintily conspicuous. How much sweeter to dry the tears that flow because one cannot accede to some demonstrable fallacy in her theory of variable stars, than to kiss her into conformity as to the dinner-hour or the fitness or unfitness of such-or-such a person to be asked to a picnic! How much more dulcet the *dulcis Amaryllidis ira* when Amaryllis knows Sophocles and Hegel by heart, than when her accomplishments extend only to a moderate proficiency in French and the pianoforte! It is a great consolation to reflect that, among all the bewildering changes to which the world is subject, the character of woman cannot be altered; and that, so long as she abstains from absolute outrages against nature—such as divided skirts, free-thinking, tricycles, and Radicalism—neither Greek, nor conic sections, nor political economy, nor cigarettes, nor athletics can ever really do other than enhance the charm of that sweet unreasonableness which humbles the gods to the dust and compels them to adore the lace below the last hem of her brocade! It is owing to this ineradicable perfection that time cannot change nor custom stale her infinite variety.

A French writer has complained that there are not more than about twenty-five species of woman. Had not his senses been Frenchified, he would have perceived that every woman is a species in herself—nay, many species. The aspects of reason are finite, but those of unreason infinite;

and, so long as one woman is left in the world, no poet can want a perfectly unspoilt subject, and one which can never be fathomed. Some poet has, with much *vraisemblance*, represented Jove as creating woman in order that there might be at least one thing in the universe that should have for him the zest of unintelligibility—which nothing but weakness and unreason could supply. The human creature, however, is incapable of the absolutely incomprehensible; therefore it has been providentially devised that no man should be without some touch of womanhood, and no woman without some manhood. Were it otherwise, they would be wholly uninteresting to one another, and could no more mix than oil and water. This reciprocal tincture of each other's sex produces that mixture of inscrutability and comprehensibility in the well-constituted and well-matched man and woman, and that endless misunderstanding, mitigated by obscure insight, which, if not the original cause of love, is the source of that perpetual agitation of the feelings which indefinitely increases love, and without which love, if it did not die, would at least go to sleep. "Fax agitando magis ardescit."

Most of the failures in marriage come of the man's not having manhood enough to assert the prerogatives which it is the woman's more or less secret delight to acknowledge. She knows her place, but does not know how to keep it unless he knows it also; and many an otherwise amiable woman grows restless and irritable under the insupportable doubt as to whether she has got her master. In order to put the question to the test, she does things she knows he is bound to resist or resent, in the hope of being put down with a high hand and perhaps a bad word or two—since even the mildest corporal chastisement has gone out with the heroic days of such lovers as Siegfried and Kriemhild.

Friendship and love differ mainly in this: that, whereas the felicity of friendship consists in a mutual interchange of benefits, intellectual and otherwise, that of love is in giving on one part and receiving on the other, with a reciprocal perception of how sweet it is to the endower to endow and the receiver to receive. This relation involves, as ancient philosophers and theologians have observed, a certain opulence on the one side and a corresponding destitution on the other—a destitution which, however, is the greatest opulence in the eyes of the former as being the necessary condition of his proper delight, which is to endow. The myth of King Cophetua and the Beggar-Maid is representative of the most perfect nuptial relationship.

All joy worth the name is in equal love between unequals; and the inmost delight of giving honour lies in its being of voluntary favour, and that of receiving it in the perception that the rendering of it is an infatuation of love on the part of the giver. Desert cares as little for honour as it is in the habit of receiving it. The vanity of a woman need not derogate from that sense of comparative nothingness which is to herself the sweetest part of the offering of her affection. Indeed, her vanity may be based upon this sense of her smallness, as knowing that this is the source of her attractiveness. A woman without the vanity which delights in her power of attracting would be by that very fact without power to attract; for she would want the power to receive that which the man delights to give—namely, that tender corroboration and consummation of her sense of her own sweetness, which every lover imagines that he of all men is alone able to confer upon her.

As to the unreason of woman, there is a positive character about it which elevates it from defect into a sort of sacred mystery. "Perhaps," says Thomas Hardy, the greatest living authority on the subject, "in no minor point does woman astonish her helpmate more than in the strange power she possesses of believing cajoleries that she knows to be false, except, indeed, in that of being utterly sceptical on strictures which she knows to be true." Philip van Artevelde says—with perfect truth as to the fact, but with a most erroneous implied inference—"How little flattering is a woman's love!" They understand little of love who do not see how great a part is played in it by mirth and paradox, and how the surprise of finding oneself loved the more for a kiss or a compliment makes up abundantly for the disappointment of discovering that the greatest merits or self-sacrifice do not count for much in comparison.

When the Father of Gods and men presented the newly created woman to the Council of Olympus, we know that she was greeted with peals of laughter; and to this day there is nothing that a woman of well-balanced mind hates more in a man than his taking her too much *au grand sérieux.*

It has been the practice of the Catholic Church not to define a dogma, nor to promulgate it as a necessary part of faith, until it has come to be widely denied; and that Church to which all truly sensible persons, be they Catholic or otherwise, belong, is ever careful to abstain from formulating doctrines so long as they continue to constitute portions of the implicit and active belief of mankind in general. Words tend to obscure and blunt the edge of truth, which is better felt than spoken; but when it is no longer generally felt, and is widely spoken against, then there is no help for it but to hurl anathemas against its deniers. Now it is high time that it should be plainly declared that there are few more damnable heresies than the doctrine of the equality of man and woman. It strikes at the root of the material and spiritual prosperity and felicity of both, and vitiates the whole life of society in its source. From time to time in the world's past history, the inferiority and consequent subordination of woman have been denied by some fanatic or insignificant sect of fanatics, and the cudgels have been taken up for man by some busybody in his premature dread of the "monstrous regiment of women"; but the consensus of the world has until lately been dead against the notion. Every man Jack would have listened with a cheery laugh at the setting up of a claim of equality on the part of his dame Jill; and Aristotle, Bacon, and St. Thomas Aquinas would have regarded with silent wonder the idea of raising to an equal rank with her lord the *placens uxor* whom the Angelical Doctor declares to be "scarcely a reasonable creature." Here and there, indeed, a "poet sage" has glorified the woman in terms that, taken literally, are violently heterodox; but everybody knew what he meant in thus making a divinity of her whose very excellence consists in her being decidedly a little lower than the angels—those transmitters of the divinity of which she is only the last reflector. Lovers, also, have in all ages practised a playful idolatry; and if they are beginning now to drop the language of hyperbole, it is because they are liable now to be believed. The ideal position of woman towards man, according to the doctrine of the Church—which, in this instance at least, is verifiable by all who have the power of psychological observation—is that of his reflection or "glory." She is the sensible glory or praise of his spiritual wisdom, as the rising cloud of incense is that of the invisible sunshine, which, passing through the painted window, becomes manifest in all its rainbow hues only when it strikes upon the otherwise colourless vapour. The world—which sometimes fancies that it is being extremely cynical when it is only expressing emphatically some Christian and philosophical verity—expresses this fact when it says that the virtue of woman is the noblest invention of man. She has not the strength for, or indeed the knowledge of, true virtue and grace of character, unless she is helped to that knowledge and strength by the man.

"He for God only, she for God in him."

She only really loves and desires to become what

he loves and desires her to be; and beauty, being visible or reflected goodness, can exist in woman only when and in proportion as the man is strong, good, and wise. When man becomes womanish, and ceases to be the transmitter of the heavenly light of wisdom, she is all abroad, she does not know what to do with herself, and begins to chatter or scream about her rights; but, in this state, she has seldom understanding enough to discern that her true right is to be well governed by right reason, and, instead of pouring contempt on her degraded companion for his spiritual impotence, she tries all sorts of hopeless tricks—the most hopeless of all being that of endeavouring to become manly—in order the better to attract him who has become womanish.

To maintain that man and woman are equals in intelligent action is just as absurd as it would be to maintain that the hand that throws a ball and the wall that casts it back are equal. The woman has an exquisite perception and power of admiring all the man can be or do. She is the "glory" of his prowess and nobility in war, statesmanship, arts, invention, and manners; and she is able to fulfil this, her necessary and delightful function, just because she is herself nothing in battle, policy, poetry, discovery, or original intellectual or moral force of any kind.

The true happiness and dignity of woman are to be sought, not in her exaltation to the level of man, but in a full appreciation of her inferiority and in the voluntary honour which every manly nature instinctively pays to the weaker vessel. In the infinite distance between God and man, theologians find the secret of the infinite felicity of divine love; and the incomparable happiness of love between the sexes is similarly founded upon their inequality. The playfulness which is the very dainty and "bouquet" of love, comes of the fact that in the mutual worship of lovers there is always a tacit understanding of something of a King Cophetua and Beggar-Maid relationship. No right-minded woman would care a straw for her lover's adoration if she did not know that he knew that after all he was the true divinity.

There is a mystic craving in the great to become the love-captive of the small, while the small has a corresponding thirst for the enthralment of the great.

" 'Tis but in such captivity
The boundless heavens know what they be."

The central prophecy in the Old Testament is that "A man shall be compassed by a woman.'

'This wonder, which is applied by the Prophet to higher things, is also the secret of human love and its marvellous order. The infinite circumscribed by the finite, the great by the small, is the insoluble paradox which teases human affection with inexhaustible delight, as it is the thought which kindles and keeps alive the devotion of the Saint.

When this order ceases to exist, and with it the life and delight of love, it is wholly the man's fault. A woman will consent to be small only when the man is great; but then she sets no bounds to her sweet self-humiliation, and by becoming the slave of his reason she reduces him to a like captivity to her desires. The widely extended impatience of women under the present condition of things is nothing but an unconscious protest against the diminished manliness of men. When a large proportion of our male population are thrilled with effeminate pain if an injury is done to the skin of a cat or of an Irish rebel, but feel no indignation or anguish at the violation of every sound principle and the deadening of every sentiment that ennobles life, women feel that the external conditions of true womanhood have disappeared; and it is not to be wondered at if many of them, unclothed, as it were, of the sentiment of surrounding manhood, should, in their ignorant discomfort and despair, make as unsightly a spectacle of themselves as does the animal called a hermit-crab when, by some chance, it is ejected, bare, comfortless, and unprotected, from the shell of its adoption.

XXI

DIEU ET MA DAME

WOMAN is the last and lowest of all spiritual creatures; made "a little lower than the angels" to be "crowned with the glory and honour" of being the final and visible reflection of the beauty of God, which in itself no eye shall ever otherwise see; for "the beatific vision," as St. Bernard says, "is not a thing that is seen, but a substance which is sucked, as through a nipple." The Blessed Virgin, "the holiest and humblest of creatures," crowned with the glory and honour of bearing God in her womb, is the one woman in whom womanhood has been perfected, and in whom the whole of womanhood has been more or less reconstituted and glorified.

But though woman has thus been glorified by an inconceivably higher circumstance of honour than man, and has been made and declared to be not only "Regina Mundi" but "Regina Cœli," man, in the order of being, is and will for ever be above her. He, as man, seems to be, in some sort, the last of the angelic order, being not only a reflection but also a transmitter and messenger of the Divine original Fatherhood, represented to the Blessed Virgin herself in St. Joseph. Theology teaches that a characteristic of all the angelic orders is the capacity of assuming a double aspect. They can turn their gaze directly upon God, a state which St. Thomas Aquinas describes as the "Morning Joy," or they can turn to God in his creature, which is said to be the "Evening Joy." The Father alone looks for ever downward, and the woman alone for ever upward, "her angel always beholding the face" of the original divinity; and, in whatever order an angelic substance may stand, all orders below and above are, as it were, transparent, the vision of each ending, in one direction, in the Father, and, in the other, in the Woman, that opaque surface in which the rays of Deity end, and from which they are reflected in all the multiplied splendours which they have gathered by being transmitted through the prismatic and refractive spheres that intervene. In this duplicate order, each angelic entity represents and contains the Divine Fatherhood for the entity next below, and the womanhood, its "glory" for that next above; a fact which Milton seems to have discerned, without the aid of Catholic theology, when he wrote

"Spirits at will
Can either sex assume;"

and which every "Bride of Christ" who is also a pure and ardent Lover discerns, when his eyes are first opened, as by a deific flash, to the feminine splendour, and he feels that "Dieu et ma Dame" is no irreverent or hyperbolic legend for his double but not divided worship. The ideal womanhood, which only one woman has realised fully, but which every woman seems to be capable of more or less representing to some man, for at least one moment in his life, is the photosphere of God, the light and joy of the universe, "Regina Mundi," as the glory of nature, and "Regina Cœli" when she shall have become nature glorified.

Man, then, as soon as he is made by grace a participator of angelic and celestial powers, stands between God and woman, and, as he pleases and when he pleases, can take aspect as Bride to Christ or bridegroom to woman, the Priestess of the Divine Truth or Beauty to him, as he is Priest of the Divine Love or Power to her.

To render this, the central fact of life, conceivable and credible to such as have not attained to knowledge, those who know have remarked certain analogies, say rather identities of Divine and human love, of which, from reading and hearing whereof I have kept no exact notes, I will give a few examples.

The doctrine of election, which is such that it can be neither accepted nor denied by the understanding, has its lively image in "the way of a man with a maid," which, also, Solomon himself confessed that he could not understand. The man sees many maids, often of much more apparent beauty and merit than the one he chooses; and, in his choice of her, there is no compulsion. He may feel attracted by somewhat in her, but he is not in love with her, until by an act of will, he abandons his will, and assumes, by a distinct act of election, a state of mind towards her from which thenceforward he is unable to withdraw himself, whereby it becomes her manifest fault if she does not "make her election sure" by offering no such violence to love as must inevitably cause divorce.

Again, the Divine Lover, like a wise mortal lover, knows well that, however favourably the Soul may be disposed to Him, by His greatness, power, wealth, goodness, and abundant benevolence to her, He must *desire* her, and give her some sensible proof by smile, touch, or caress, which shall say to her heart, as the God of David says to the chosen, "Rex concupiscet decorem tuum."

Again, God's strength, like man's, is perfected in weakness. When the Soul has entered upon her third and crowning stage of perfection and union, His divine weakness for her gives Him far more influence over her will than would be obtained by any display of His power and other attributes. As with a mortal lover, there is, as some one has said, an appearance of infatuation in the love of God for the elect soul. Though just and beneficent to others, He has nothing but boundless indulgence for her. "If she loves," says Saint Augustine, "she may do as she likes." He will forgive her, almost without asking, all faults short of wilful and persistent infidelity, and, since she herself hates them, He even loves her the more for them. What ardent lover but knows that the present faults and shortcomings of the beloved are condiments and excitations of the appetite of love, impediments in the current of his passion which only render its self-willed and self-rejoicing force more sensible and triumphant? And past corruptions that are really past and no longer active are so far from hindering love that they act as manure in which the seed of Divine Love and the seed almost divine of a pure and fervid mortal affection flourish wonderfully, many a Magdalen, the just envy of many who were always pure, having been formed into a spouse, "more innocent than any maid," by the inveterate and purifying ardour of either love.

Again, as with a mortal lover, God does not require any service of external "charity," etc., from His beloved. Indeed, He complains, as He did to Martha, of all attempts to please Him otherwise than by giving Him her society and her person in contemplation. "All," says St. Francis of Sales, "must serve her" (the elect Soul), "but she must serve none, not even her Divine Lover, of whom she is not a servant but a spouse." He reproves in her the kind of humility which He requires of others, in whom He has not yet inspired that perfection of intention which in her He regards as attainment. He also requires in her, as a mortal lover does, that amount of "vanity," as the world calls it, which sees and rejoices in her own beauty; for it is only her knowledge of her own loveliness in His eyes which makes His love credible to her, and it is only her belief in His love which enables her to give that perfect response of feeling which is love's fruition, and causes her beauty to brighten more and more in the joy of His flatteries, making her "sweet to herself who is so sweet to Him."

Again, in either love, the one party retains a

power of absolute command, which he never uses, while the other has an equal force of persuasion, of which she avails herself abundantly. She delights in calling herself his slave; he delights in being hers, and in boasting himself a "servant of servants."

A mysterious longing for corporeal and spiritual captivity to the beloved animates either kind of love—if, indeed, they be not really one in kind. In love, the woman, who is "the body," desires to be utterly captive to the man's will, and he, in return, to be utterly captive to her body. His soul lives in and is moved blissfully by every turn of her head and motion of her limbs. He already is carried hither and thither in all her movements, although he is not yet *numerically* one flesh with her; but this is much more so with the Divine Lover, who actually enjoys that distinctness in identity to which the mortal lover only and for ever in vain aspires, namely, to be "man compassed by a woman," as Isaiah says, speaking of that Incarnation which is effected more or less in each of the elect, as in Jesus Himself perfectly. These two captivities constitute one freedom, and every look and gesture of the beloved is a sacrament and a common joy. As I have said elsewhere—

"'Tis but in such captivity
The heavens themselves know what they be."

Another remarkable point in this divine analogy is the reciprocal desire of the great for the small and the small for the great. An ordinary man requires in his mistress abilities corresponding to his own, and he who cannot love much commonly demands from her a great power of love for him. A great man has a wilful and somewhat amused delight ("Olli subridens") in binding himself in wedlock to one who, indeed, implicitly believes in his greatness, but who is really nothing but a little, ignorant Love, who gives all her mite and understands only caresses. To a great man and to a God a little love is a great thing. As the greatest of souls is infinitely little to God, it follows that this peculiar source of felicity in extremes is, in the divine marriage, unfathomable and inexhaustible.

Another phenomenon common to both kinds of love is the longing—almost the first that arises in every true lover's bosom—to die for the sake of the beloved. "I have longed for this hour," said Our Lord. But none, save God, can die and yet live for her.

Again, between lovers, things which, under ordinary relationships, are only "counsels of perfection," become obligatory duties; the least inattention is almost a mortal offence, raising a cloud of separation which nothing but bitter penance and greater devotion than ever can dissipate; so that the spouse of God may well suspect the reality of her position, if her life, in this world, is not fuller of sorrows than of smiles, and if her failures have not rendered her perfection sensibly greater this week than it was last.

Again, in human as in divine love, "a part is greater than the whole," and either love finds its fruition in sacraments or symbols, which are parts representing the whole. Even in the presence of the beloved, the lover will choose to fix his soul upon a ribbon or a lock of hair, intensifying his apprehension of a too numerous and overwhelming beauty by thus focusing it on one point. Another of the many paradoxes common to both loves is, that they can see best in the dark. "Night is the light of my pleasures."

Again, since, in this life, the wedlock of God and the soul is, at best, only in its first stage or betrothal, its felicities, to the soul at least, are, as with the betrothed maiden, defective, full of unintelligible and impatient desires, and daily mingled with the almost intolerable miseries of temporary separation, which seems eternal; for, while it lasts, she cannot see her own beauty, which exists for her only in the light of His countenance. When thus He withdraws from her, she becomes in her own eyes vile, unmeaning, and unlovely as the sheath of a lost sword, or the cast skin of a serpent, and it is impossible at such times to give a sensible belief to the certainty that she will, ere long, be again alive with His life and splendid with the reflection of His complacency.

Another most notable analogy of love is the revelation, completion, and explanation of herself which the lover in either case brings to the beloved. She is as the fragment of a "puzzle-picture," until she encounters the destined complement of her being, and the key to her unintelligible dreams. They then suddenly become such realities as make all other realities dreams. She dares not believe or accept the wonders of her position until she discerns that acceptance of them is imposed on her by duty and faith. Then she can no more doubt that, through all the range of her constitution, she is the blissful reciprocal of him whom she adores, than she could doubt of her own existence, which, indeed, without him, would now be no existence. In him is the only possible satisfaction of her rational, voluntary, and sensitive life, and she attains to fathomless content in the extremes of reverence for and intimacy with him.

But this is perhaps the greatest and most inscrutable of all the mysteries common to either kind of love—there is, in its felicity, the coexistence of a celestial and exceedingly virginal pride with an insatiable appetite for its surrender and sacrifice. Theologians say that the essential of the Sacrifice of the Altar is the infinite humiliation suffered by the Second Person of the Holy Trinity in becoming flesh in the moment of transubstantiation; and has not this humiliation its analogue in the case of the Virgin when she allows her love and beauty, thitherto nothing but spiritual splendour and ethereal freedom, to become the ally and thrall of the body?

The last of the innumerable analogies, or rather identities, which I shall here notice is the indissolubility of union, when it has reached its final stage. So long as love in the soul is only in the initial state of light, or assent to and admiration of what is most excellent, the light may be quenched by other lights, less pure and bright, but nearer; when, again, the light descends into the will, this may not be able to bear the strain of a love that calls for continual fidelity of correspondence; but when it reaches the sensible affections and has been crowned in mutual and ineffable complacencies, there is no longer any practical danger of separation. The Soul feels assured that, above and apart from the great security she enjoys in the fact that all temptation has been cut up at the roots by her possession of a sensible and abiding felicity which makes all others insipid, and which enables her to say, with full sincerity, "Whom have I in Heaven but Thee, and what on earth in comparison with Thee," her Lord also has entered into new relations with her, and she is relieved of obligations, while He has assumed them. He wants nothing of her now which she does not delight to give; whereas He has taken on Him the marital duty of seeing that all temptation which could endanger her is kept at a distance; He is bound to cherish and comfort, and behave, not with justice, but with tender indulgence to His own flesh; and, in case of any occasional weakness of obedience on her part, to show Himself the loving Master that she loves Him to be, by *compelling* her sensitive disinclination to such external duties as may remain. He has now made her "holy" or "separate" to Himself, and "He will not suffer His Holy One to see corruption." His mercies are now "the *sure* mercies of David," and though she acknowledges that there is still a hypothetical possibility of divorce should she fall, as it is practically incredible that she now can, a possibility that causes her to "rejoice with trembling," yet, on the whole, she is "*sure* that neither death, nor life, nor angels, nor principalities, nor powers, nor things present, nor things to come, nor height, nor depth, nor any other creature," shall be able to separate her from her Love.

This parallel appears to fail in one point; I mean, the extreme jealousy on the part of the Divine Lover of the Soul, when once she has entered upon this relationship to Him, and the entire absence of jealousy on her part. Sleep and accidental and external duty do not separate her from Him, but the least waking thought, feeling, word, or act, which has not Him, directly or indirectly, for its object, does. When God makes Himself as wine to the Beloved, like the fabled Bacchus, the one thing He resents is inattention, and when she has fallen into this offence, she has to recover her favour with Him by tears and prayers. She, however, is not only content but delighted to think that there are many whom He loves as well as or better than He loves her. I attribute this fact to her instinctive perception that her beauty is unique ("there is none like her, none"), and that no other can ever be to Him what she is, though millions may be a great deal more. Moreover, by virtue of the supernatural elevation of her intellect in her intimacies with Him, she is enabled to discern that He has the power of absolutely forgetting all others when she is in His presence, and that He is, at such times, wholly hers; a concrete fact which the philosophers express in the abstract, when they affirm that "God is a circle whose centre is everywhere and circumference nowhere."

Perhaps—but I am not sure, for I do not know the mind of women or that of the Saints well enough to judge—the parallel also fails in this, that, in the higher relationship, the soul is always more or less troubled by the incredibility of so much bliss and honour, and, in the presence of the only reality of life, a reality as natural as it is spiritual, she perpetually sighs—

> "Ah, me, I do not dream,
> Yet all this does some heathen fable seem!"

With these exceptions, if exceptions they be, there is, indeed, *no* vital characteristic of a perfectly ordered love in the natural sphere, which has not its likeness and full development in the Divine; nor can even the natural perfection of love be attained without habitual reference to the spiritual. Wordsworth says:

> "By grace divine,
> Not otherwise, O Nature, are we thine,"

and a man can only love a woman with full felicity by understanding and obeying Christ's injunction that he should love her as He loves the Church, which every lover of God is in little, "The woman for the man," "the man by the woman," and "God all in all" in both:—for Milton's rule,

"He for God only, she for God in him,"

is not a wholly adequate statement of the relationship of man and woman, though it is as near a statement as a Socinian could be expected to arrive at. The woman is "homo" as well as the man, though one element, the male, is suppressed and quiescent in her, as the other, the female, is in him; and thus he becomes the Priest and representative to her of the original Fatherhood, while she is made to him the Priestess and representative of that original Beauty which is "the express image and glory of the Father," each being equally, though not alike, a manifestation of the Divine to the other.

Love, with this commentary on it written in the hearts of lovers, becomes as much brighter, purer, and more ardent than the love which is without it as the electric light is brighter, purer, and more ardent than a torch of tar; and so far is it from being true, as the foolish might imagine, that something of the natural delight of love must be lost in this its exaltation, that everything which is truly in Nature's order gains immensely by the supernatural heat and light which illuminate and purge the exceeding obscurity of the phenomena of the uninformed natural passion.

Should any believing reader object that such thoughts as I have suggested to him imply an irreverent idea of the intimacies of God with His elect, I beg him to remember that in receiving the Blessed Sacrament with the faith which the Church demands, he affirms and *acts* a familiarity which is greater than any other that can be conceived.[1]

If any one perseveres in the path of perfection, these points of likeness between Divine and human love will become *res cognita et visa;* and he will see that the phenomena of the human relationship of love are such because they are the realities of the Divine. For all properly human instincts are no other than the lineaments of God; and man (*homo*) is an image and likeness of God, most especially in those mysteries which—let all remark well—are quite as inscrutable in their secondary, or human, as in their primary manifestation, "the surest foundation of marriage-love being," as Hooker says, " that of which we are least able to render a reason."

[1] For more of these analogies the reader may consult the verses called " De Natura Deorum," in the *Unknown Eros*.

Let none who have as yet had no experience of these things, though they may have been doing their very best, despair. We must usually feed for many years upon divine things before God gives us the taste of our food; and even when we have done all, we may not find ourselves among the blessed number of those who are called to the Counsels of Perfection and the fruition of God in this life.

THE END

Printed by R. & R. CLARK, LIMITED, *Edinburgh.*

www.ingramcontent.com/pod-product-compliance
Lightning Source LLC
Chambersburg PA
CBHW032153160426
43197CB00008B/898